The Archpriest of Hita and the
Imitators of Ovid

The Archpriest of Hita and the Imitators of Ovid: A Study in the Ovidian Background of the *Libro de buen amor*

by
RICHARD BURKARD

Juan de la Cuesta
Newark, Delaware

010137

Table of Contents

Acknowledgment

I wish to express my gratitude to the College of Liberal Arts at Penn State University for providing the released time necessary for the preparation of this study.

Dedicated to
MARLENE ELISABETH
for her Encouragement and Patience

Preface

THE PRESENCE OF AN Ovidian inspiration in the *Libro de buen amor* is undeniable. As we know, the Archpriest mentions Ovid a number of times and has much to say that corresponds, if only loosely and vaguely, to various passages in the *Ars amatoria*. And yet relatively little has been written about the *Libro–Ars* relationship. Rudolph Schevill, to be sure, took up the matter and so did Felix Lecoy. But Schevill's essay (a chapter in his *Ovid and the Renascence in Spain*) tends to lack for substance, and Lecoy's essay (a chapter in his *Recherches sur le* Libro de buen amor), though not without insight, is misleading in several key respects.

Nonetheless, for many decades Lecoy's comments were regarded as the final word. Scholar after scholar who had occasion to touch upon the Ovidian background of the *Libro* would simply repeat the French critics's contention that the Archpriest knew the *Ars amatoria* directly and had recourse to it for the lover's precepts in the Spanish poem. Even a commentator of the stature of Joan Corominas endorsed the approach.

It may be time, however, for a reevaluation. As we shall see in the pages to come the Archpriest probably knew nothing of Ovid's guide to seduction. Indeed, he probably knew nothing of any authentic work of the Roman poet. More likely is that his knowledge was limited to certain imitative compositions which circulated in the West during the later Middle Ages.

But to concentrate solely on determining the identity of our poet's sources would be to ignore the equally important aspect of social relevance. Much can be said. Imitative Ovidian literature, for example, is clerical literature par excellence. Thus when the protagonist in the *Pamphilus* seeks out an unscrupulous go–between to aid him in a seduction he is making use of a personage held in special esteem by the clergy for the arrangement of sexual encounters. Likewise when "Ovid" in the *Pseudo–Ars amatoria* suggests the lover avoid speaking to his lady up close and communicate instead from a distance, the purpose goes beyond a simple promotion of modesty.

A good deal can also be said about literary value. In the *De amore* of Andreas Capellanus, for example, the content of Book Three or the antilove development is often banal and monotonous. On the other hand, the *Pamphilus* stands out as a work of art. In the 390 distichs comprising the piece one perceives the true frivolous spirit of Ovid combined with a pathos equally on a level with that of the Master. There is even a degree of universality: in its way this "elegiac comedy" conveys the plight of many a person whose sexual passion is frustrated by conventional restraints. The Archpriest drew upon good literature when he converted the story into the central episode of his "autobiography."

But first things first. Before getting into specifics we would find it informative to have a look at the general run of imitative Ovidiana written in Latin, especially Ovidiana relating to the *Ars amatoria*.[1] This will be done in Chapter One.

---

[1] There is no hard evidence that our poet drew from imitative literature composed in the vernacular.

I
The *Ars Amatoria* and the Latin Middle Ages

ÆTAS OVIDIANA, THE AGE OF Ovid, was the name given by Ludwig Traube to the 12th century.[1] The designatiom is apt. From roughly the middle of the 11th century till several decades into the 13th the works of the Roman poet were a general object of study in the schools of England, France, and Germany. Few were the scholars at the time who had no knowledge of his verse.

It would be inaccurate, however, to suppose that earlier centuries were also familiar with his poetry. Indeed, the great popularity of Ovid during the 12th century came about only after a long period of eclipse. At times and in places he even appears to have been unknown. In a poem of Alcuin (second half of the eighth century), for example, in which there is reference to the authors in the library at York there is not a single mention of Ovid.[2]

This neglect of the Augustan writer was not peculiar to the early Middle Ages. Already in the last few centuries of Antiquity his works were being read less and less. One can understand why: interest in a creation like the *Ars amatoria*, a poetic guide to philandering, requires a level of civilization which was ceasing to exist in the West from the third century on. In addition, the advance

---

[1] Ludwig Traube, *Einleitung in die lateinische Philologie des Mittelalters*, p. 113. For an outline of the generality of Ovidian literature in the Middle ages see the entry contributed by Richard Dwyer to the *Dictionary of the Middle Ages*, vol. 9, pp. 312–14.

[2] There is however mention of Virgil, Lucan, and Statius. Cf. L. P. Wilkinson, *Ovid Recalled*, p. 373.

of a rigorously ascetic religion, as was the Christianity of the period, was bound to foment a cultural milieu having little use for Ovidian sensuality.[3]

Still another factor contributing to the neglect of Ovid was a preference for Virgil. The latter was the greatest of the "patriotic" poets, the bard who sang of the origin of the Roman people and glorified their virtues. In an age of collapse like the fifth and sixth centuries it was quite natural that the preferred artist should be the one who did the most to justify the *pax romana*. And later, in the so called Carolingian Era, when much of the West was governed by a ruler who pretended to restore the empire of Rome, what, again, was more natural than that the literati should hold in high regard the imperial poet par excellence. If Traube called the 12th century the *ætas Ovidiana*, he rightly called the ninth century the *ætas Virgiliana*, the age of Virgil.[4]

But with the coming of the 11th century the economic and political situation began to change. Trade and commerce were on the increase, cities were growing, the social order was becoming more complex. The new circumstance created a need, as one might expect, for greater and more diversified education. For this task the inherited monastic schools, the majority of schools that existed during the preceding period, were inadequate. To make up for the deficiency the so called cathedral schools or the instructional establishments attached to the principal sites of church government took on importance. With time some of these became prominent as centers of learning, especially the ones located at Chartres and

---

[3] To get an idea of the degree of asceticism prevalent among Christians in the first several centuries A.D. one need only consider that church leaders sometimes advocated the expulsion of widows or widowers who sought to remarry. Obviously these were people unlikely to be Ovid enthusiasts.

[4] Traube, p. 113. Still another factor contributing to the popularity of Virgil —the same one having a detrimental effect on Ovid— was religious piety. In spite of the clearly pagan tenor of the Mantuan's poetry the notion was widespread that he had been a seer who foresaw the coming of Christianity. Behind this belief lay the fourth *Eclogue* which seemed to convey a prediction of the birth of Christ. Here was a poet hard to surpass.

Orleans in France. The kind of education offered to students was still intended to meet ecclesiastical needs. But even so, it was more secular in content than that provided by the monks and the monasteries. Above all, there was an emphasis on the "classics," including the works of Ovid, as had not been the case for centuries. In a catalog of suitable readings, for example, prepared by the French grammarian Aimeric (second half of the 11th century), we find the poet ranked among the "aurei auctores," the nine authors considered authoritative in their respective topics.[5] A formidable change in outlook had set in.

Ovid's "arrival" did not mean, however, that all resistance to the reading of his works was at an end: there were still prominent churchmen who understood the character of pagan poetry and saw fit to object. Alexander of Villedieu (late 12th, early 13th centuries) had this to say about the study of non–Christian literature:[6]

> Sacrificare deis nos edocet Aurelianis
> Indicens festum Fauni Iovis atque Liei.
> Hec est pestifera, David testante, cathedra,
> In qua non sedet vir sanctus, perniciosam
> Doctrinam fugiens, que, sicut habetur ibidem,
> Est quasi diffundens multis contagia morbus.
> Non decet illa legi que sunt contraria legi.

(The school at Orleans instructs us to sacrifice to the gods and points out the festivals of Faunus, Jove, and Bacchus. This is a pestilent seat of learning in which, as David bears witness, the holy man will not sit down, but chooses rather to flee the harmful teaching. The instruction given there is like a contagious disease that spreads among the crowds. Nothing should be read that is contrary to the [divine] law.)

---

[5] Cf. E. R. Curtius, *European Literature and the Latin Middle Ages*, pp. 464–65.

[6] Quoted as in Louis John Paetow, *The Arts Course at Medieval Universities with Special Reference to Grammar and Rhetoric*, p. 21. All translations here and throughout are those of the present writer unless otherwise indicated.

Needed, then, for the study of Ovid and other pagan authors was some form of theological or moralistic justification. This was readily had with resort to the time honored tradition of the allegorical exposition, i.e., an exegesis according to which a given text was thought to contain two kinds of meaning, the one, an obvious meaning to be determined from the literal sense of words or expressions, and the other, a symbolic or hidden meaning to be determined upon reflection.

Commentaries on Ovidian poetry along these lines soon came to abound.[7] For a forthright example we might consider the following hexameters (12th century, anonymous) composed, it seems, by a cleric for the edification of nuns:[8]

> Quid culpare soles, quod amat nunc carnea proles,
> et mortale genus, quid ob hoc culpare solemus?
> vos notat et clerum tam mystica fabula rerum;
> abbatissarum genus et grex omnis earum
> sunt Pallas plane, tria virginis ora Dianæ,
> Juno, Venus, Vesta, Thetis; observantia vestra
> est expressa satis cultu tantæ deitatis.
> vos notat istarum genus et gens sacra dearum:
> nos ratione pari divum deitate notari
> credimus, et cleri typus illa videtur haberi
> inclita magnorum series memorata deorum
> nos qui virtutis opus ardua vota salutis,
> et canonum scita sectamur celibe vita,
> cum deliremus, ea numina significamus.

[Why does one often find fault with the presence of [sexual] love in the carnal offspring of a mortal species? Why do we often find fault with this? A mystical tale of similar events signifies you [the nuns] and the clergy: Minerva is clearly a figure of the type of the abbess and all her flock, as is also the virgin Diana, she of three aspects, and Juno, Venus, Vesta and

---

[7] For the interpretation of Ovid in this fashion see the article of Lester K. Born, "Ovid and Allegory."

[8] Quoted as in Born, p. 372.

Thetis. Yes, your religious practice is clearly indicated by the worship of such deities. The type of these goddesses and their holy adherents refers to you. And we believe with like reasoning that we [the clergy] are signified by the male gods, and our type seems to be equivalent to that famous and memorable array of great divinities. We are those who pursue works of virtue along with a rigorous dedication to salvation in accord —as is proper— with the celibacy decreed by law. When we feel inspiration, we show symbolically the power of the gods.]

Not everyone went this far. Some educators simply made a selection, recommending for study those works considered useful and rejecting those considered harmful. Thus the author of the *Sacerdos ad altare* sets forth a group of readings thought to be of value (including some by Ovid) but cautions against another group thought to be unduly provocative. In connection with the second evaluation he writes:[9]

> Placuit tamen viris autenticis carmina amatoria cum satiris subducenda esse a manibus adolescentium, ac si eis dicitur:
> "Qui legitis flores et humi nascencia fraga,
> frigidus, o pueri, fugite hinc, latet anguis in herba."

> (It seemed well to men of authority that love poems and satirical pieces ought to be removed from the hands of young people, as if to say to them: "You boys who gather flowers and fresh strawberries from the ground, flee from there; a cold snake lies in wait amidst the green.")

And yet all the amatory works of Ovid enjoyed a wide circulation. Indeed, not only were they read and expounded upon in the schools, but became an object of imitation as well. One could even speak of a "classroom industry" turning out verses modeled on those of the Master. Many such pieces amounted, as we might suppose, to a lineup of metrified words with little æsthetic value.

---

[9] As in Paetow, p. 23.

Some, however, demonstrate a combination of sexuality and religious convention worthy of note. The following distichs afford a good example (we are treated to a dialog between a nun and a young man):[10]

> Te mihi meque tibi genus, ætas et decor æquant:
> cur non ergo sumus sic in amore pares?
>
> hac non veste places: aliis nigra vestis ametur;
> quæ nigra sunt fugio, candida semper amo.
>
> si vestem fugias, niveam tamen aspice carnem
> et sub veste nigra candida crura pete.
>
> nupsiste Christo, quem non offendere fas est:
> hoc velum sponsam te probat esse Dei.
>
> deponam velum, deponam cetera quæque,
> ibit et ad lectum nuda puella tuum.
>
> ut velo careas, tamen altera non potes esse,
> et mea culpa minus non foret inde gravis.
>
> culpa quidem, sed culpa levis foret ista: fatemur
> hoc fore peccatum, sed veniale tamen.
>
> uxorem violare viri, grave crimen habetur:
> est gravius sponsam me violare Dei.
>
> vicisti nostrum sancta ratione furorem:
> gaudeo quod verbis sum superata tuis.

(We are like each other in type, age, and taste. Why, then, should we not be united in love?

---

[10] Quoted as in F. J. E. Raby, *A History of Secular Latin Poetry in the Middle Ages*, I, p. 354.

You don't appeal to me in that clothing: any woman who is dressed in black will have to get love from someone else; those in black I stay away from; my love is only for those in white.

If it's my dress you avoid, just look at my white flesh; beneath the black garb are white legs; come and take them.

You're married to Christ; it's not right to offend Him. The veil proves you belong to God as his spouse.

I'll take off the veil. I'll take off everything else too. You'll have me, a naked girl, in your bed.

Even though you get rid of your veil, you cannot be different from what you are. And the guilt I'll incur will not be less.

Guilt there is, yes, but it would be slight. I admit doing this is a sin, but it's a minor one.

To violate a man's wife is considered a serious offense. It would be even more serious to violate a spouse of God.

You've overcome my passion with your saintly persuasion. You talked me out of it; I'm glad.)

An unabashed compound of the sacred and the licentious! But there is method to the madness: one has the impression that the religious–moralizing element (out and out artificial in the final couplet) serves primarily to neutralize objections from an eventual censor. The author amused himself by having the nun speak as she does, but at the same time made certain the piece contained adequate counterstatements to protect its existence. The procedure is not unique: it turns up repeatedly in Ovidian inspired compositions where the writer —including our Archpriest of Hita— apparently thought a risqué theme would be incomplete without the addition of a palliative.

Though cleverly composed the dialog between the nun and the

young man is short on artistic worth: important for the poet was a
demonstration of academic proficiency. And such is the case, as
already indicated, with much of this versifying. There were,
however, a few persons of talent who passed through the schools
and eventually built up a literary corpus of value. Especially
prominent are Hildebert of Lavardin, Marbod of Rennes, and Baudry
de Bourgueil, all of whom flourished in the second half of the 11th
century. As some of their poetry is illustrative of the type of
composition that became current in imitative Ovidiana it would be
useful to have a look at a few excerpts.[11] The following couplets
from a satirical piece by Hildebert will serve for starters:[12]

> femina mente Parim, vita spoliavit Uriam
> et pietate David et Salomona fide;
> femina sustinuit iugulo damnare Johannem,
> Hippolytum letho compedibus Joseph.

(A woman deprived Paris of his sanity, Uriah of his life, David
of his piety, and Solomon of his faith. A woman caused John the
Baptist to be punished with the blade, Hippolytus to perish, and
Joseph to be thrown into shackles.)

Another compound of the holy and the unholy with the latter now
consisting in references to pagan mythology. F. J. E. Raby puts it
well when he says this sort of mixing "came naturally to men who
knew their Ovid as well as their Bible by heart."[13] But Hildebert's
satirical mode was not limited to the ravages of lust. Elsewhere, in
a different poem he bewails the general state of mores. The follow-

---

[11] For the sake of a definition we may understand the expression
"imitative Ovidian literature" as referring to the aggregate of literary themes
and motifs based —if only partially and indirectly— on those of the Roman
poet. In addition, if a piece was written in elegiac couplets or dactylic
hexameter, its Ovidian character was enhanced. But there are no limitations
as to form: one can point to an imitative composition written in prose.

[12] As in Raby, I, p. 320.

[13] Raby, I, p. 320.

ing couplets provide a sample:[14]

> destituit terras decus orbis, gloria rerum,
> virtus, mortali dicta negare mori.
> non hanc in quoquam spondet flos indolis usquam;
> scis, nihil est pietas, nominis umbra fides.
> si cœlum staret, si sol lucere negaret,
> si nix ferveret, frigida flamma foret,
> non sic pallerem, non sic mirando stuperem,
> quam si nunc usquam quemque pium videam.

(Gone from the world is a sense of dignity, a desire for renown, a true manhood which refuses to become extinct in the common way. A promise of excellence turns up in no one. Surely you must know: good character counts for nothing; loyalty is a mere word. If the heavens were to stand still, if the sun denied its light, if snow were warm, if a flame were cold, I would be no more amazed, I would be no more astonished, than if I saw someone nowadays who had integrity.)

To the modern reader a social critique along these lines may seem like a painful banality. But the theme was popular in the high Middle Ages and sometimes appeared in the form of a so–called "Complaint against the Power of Money," a sharp, resentful diatribe directed at venality, especially the venality of the church. Our Spanish poet himself was to compose a version.

Turning then to Marbod of Rennes, we might take a look at some verses quoted from a composition which tells of the course of human life):[15]

> prætereo cunas, pannorum fœda relinquo;
> infantum fletus, nutricum sperno labores.
> ad pueri propero lacrymas, quem verbere sævo
> iratus cogit dictata referre magister,

---

[14] As in Raby, I, p. 321.
[15] As in Raby, I, p. 335.

dediscenda docens quæ confinxere pœtæ,
stupra nefanda Iovis, seu Martis adultera facta,
lascivos recitans iuvenes, turpesque puellas,
mutua quos iunxit sed detestanda voluptas.
imbuit ad culpam similem rude fabula pectus,
præventusque puer vitii ferventis odore
iam cupit exemplo committere fœda deorum.

(I shall omit infancy and pass over dirty diapers and wailing babies. The duties of the wet nurse I shall disregard. I hasten on to the tears of the young lad whom the severe and angry teacher beats and forces to give a recitation. But the teaching deals with things invented by poets and best forgotten: the awful debauchery of Jupiter and the adulterous deeds of Mars. The lesson has to do with lustful young men and shameless girls whom a mutual and detestable lust has brought together. The myths fill the boy's immature mind with an inclination to sin in a similar way. Soon enticed and overcome by a wicked passion, he is eager to follow the example of the gods and commit foul deeds.)

Marbod objects, as we see, to sexual immorality in the curriculum. Nonetheless, he will go on to develop his theme making use of details characterized by Raby as "hardly possible to quote."[16] Once again, then, we have the mixing of incompatible elements. In this case, however, there is an additional factor of interest: the presence of autobiography. The passage quoted deals with the kind of education a typical school boy of the times had to endure. But is this not the same schooling to which Marbod himself had been subjected? Nowhere does he indicate that he is speaking of an unusual event or a person different from himself. It would seem the reader is being treated to a facet of the poet's own life.

This resort to the personal (whether real or feigned) turns up frequently in medieval verse modeled on that of Ovid. For the sake of an example composed by an author freely referring to himself as

---

[16] Raby, I, p. 335. For the remainder see Migne's *Patrologia latina*, CLXXI, col. 1695. The poem contains a rather graphic description of autoeroticism in the pupil as a consequence of his reading assignments.

"I," we might consider the following couplets addressed by Baudry of Bourgueil to a lady friend who was apparently a nun:[17]

> crede mihi, credasque volo, credantque legentes,
>   in te me nunquam fœdus adegit amor.
> in te concivem volo vivere virginitatem,
>   in te confringi nolo pudicitiam.
> tu virgo, vir ego, iuvenis sum, junior es tu;
>   iuro per omne quod est: nolo vir esse tibi.
> nolo vir esse tibi neque tu sis femina nobis;
>   os et cor nostram firmet amicitiam.
> pectora iungantur, sed corpora semoveantur.
>   sit pudor in facto, sit iocus in calamo.

(Believe me, I want you and my readers to believe me, an unclean love never drove me to you. I want you to maintain a proper decency; it is not my intention to destroy your modesty. You are a young woman, I am a man; I am young, you are even younger. I swear by all that is, I do not intend to deal with you in the way of men. I do not want to show masculine attention to you; I do not want you to show feminine attention to me. Let our hearts and words demonstrate our friendship. Let our feelings be together, but our bodies separate. Let there be modesty in what we do and wit in what we write.)

Baudry makes his feelings clear: what he wants is strictly a platonic relationship. Possibly his condition as a churchman had something to do with the motivation.[18] Honorable intentions, however, did not deter him from composing a hyperbolic description of his lady's physical charms. The passage has relevance; it runs as follows:[19]

---

[17] As in Raby, I, p. 343. That the woman was a nun is evident from another piece addressed to her by the poet (numbered CCIV [vv. 13–4] in Phyllis Abrahams' edition of Baudry's works entitled *Les Œuvres poétiques de Baudri de Bourgueil*).

[18] All three, Hildebert, Marbod, and Baudry were ecclesiastics of high rank.

[19] As in Raby, I, p. 343–44.

non rutilat Veneris tam clara binomia stella,
    quam rutilant ambo lumina clara tibi.
crinibus inspectis fulvum minus arbitror aurum,
    colla nitent plusquam lilia, nixve recens,
dentes plus ebore, Pario plus marmore candent,
    spirat et in labiis gratia viva tuis.
labra tument modicum; color et calor igneus illis,
    quæ tamen ambo decens temperies foveat.
iure rosis malas præponi dico tenellas,
    quas rubor et candor vestit et omne decus.
corporis ut breviter complectar composituram,
    est corpus talem quod deceat faciem.
ipsa Iovem summum posses deducere cælo,
    de Iove si verax fabula Græca foret.
in quascumque velis se formas effigiasset,
    si tua te sæclis tempora præstiterint.

(The star of Venus, the star with two names, is not as radiant as your two bright eyes. Gold I judge less yellow than your hair when I gaze upon it. Your neck is whiter than a lily or fresh snow; your teeth are more resplendent than ivory or Parisian marble. A vibrant charm exudes from your lips. Indeed, your lips are full to perfection. They have the color and warmth of a fire; and yet both are properly delicate. Your dainty cheeks, I would declare, are justly preferred to roses; they are flush with redness, with brightness, and all manner of charm. For the sake of brevity about the makeup of your body I shall say it is such as corresponds to your face. You could bring down Jupiter from heaven if the tales about Jupiter were only true. If the age in which you live could make a show of you to other ages, [your body] would make as strong an impression as you would have it do.)

In reality the theme is far from unique and corresponds to a fixed type of composition often styled a *descriptio pulchritudinis feminæ*, or a description of an ideal woman written in accordance with rhetorical guidelines (one began, for example, with the head and proceeded on down).[20] But the poet could introduce personal modifications as well. And so we see that Baudry restricts himself to a discreet generalization when he arrives at the lady's torso. His reticence was not, however, de rigueur: various other writers who composed a *descriptio* —among them our own Archpriest— did not fail to include specifics.

At this point —having had a look at a fair number of samples— we might take stock of certain thematic and compositional traits which tend to recur in imitative Ovidian literature. They are as follows:

1. A combining or juxtaposing of the sacred and the profane.
2. A promotion, whether in earnest or not, of sexual promiscuity.
3. A satirical portrayal of prevailing social and ecclesiastical conditions.
4. A presentation of themes, especially certain standard themes, in accordance with rhetorical guidelines.
5. A resort to parody and the farcical.
6. A resort, whether real or pretended, to personal experience and the autobiographic.

The above traits, as one will notice, can be found in Ovid's poetry itself.[21] The difference, then, between the themes of the Augustan writer and those of his medieval imitators is more often a matter of social circumstance than of attitude or purpose. The distinction is especially important for a proper understanding of several 12th century imitations of the *Ars amatoria*. To suppose that the authors naively overlooked the Roman poet's satirical vein in order to concentrate on the strictly pragmatic would be inaccurate. What they sought was to modernize the work by rewriting both the satire and the instructional aspect in a manner that would have greater appeal to a contemporary "inside" audience, an

---

[20] For the particulars of this sort of theme see E. Faral, *Les Arts poétiques du XIIᵉ et du XIIIᵉ siècle*, pp. 75–81.

[21] But Ovid could not, of course, have satirized church officials or affairs. Also he was too good a poet to have adhered rigorously to rhetorical norms.

ecclesiastical audience.[22] Whether they succeeded from an artistic point of view is another matter.

Among these *Ars* imitations the first and foremost —the first and foremost of all Latin recreations of Ovid's amatory verse— was the 12th century *Pamphilus* (anonymous, though often ascribed to the Roman poet in the later Middle Ages), an ensemble of some 390 distichs usually categorized under the rubric "elegiac comedy."[23]

Broadly considered the sense of the poem may be described as a brief theory of love followed by a fictional narrative serving to illustrate the practice. A summary of the plot would be useful: Pamphilus, the protagonist, is smitten with love for Galathea, a woman who lives in his vicinity. At a loss how to win her affection he calls upon the love goddess, Venus, for help. The latter appears to him and goes on to recite a pertinent *ars amandi*. Later, after the departure of the goddess, he encounters the beloved in a public place and strikes up a conversation in which he reveals his sentiments. She objects to what he has to say —though not without indicating a degree of amenability— and soon hurries off.

He then resolves to engage a go–between (to do so had been part of the advice in Venus' *ars amandi*) and gets in touch with a shrewd, quick talking old woman known for her activity on behalf of lovers. She agrees to mediate, but only after receiving a promise of payment.

The go–between sets about her task by approaching Galathea and singing the praises of Pamphilus. She also speaks highly of an amatory relationship and the possibility of marriage. Galathea expresses concern about harm to her reputation, but the go–between assures her that everything can be kept under cover. Obvious from

---

[22] In the *Ars*, for example, the go–between does not play a special role. But she does in many of the imitations. She is in fact a key personage. One can understand why: a tendency among the clergy to value secrecy in a sexual affaire.

[23] All references to the *Pamphilus* correspond to the edition of Franz G. Becker (Pamphilus, *Prolegomena zum* Pamphilus *und kritische Textausgabe*.) The term "elegiac comedy" can be misleading: it seems unlikely that these pieces (mostly middle size in length and cast in dramatic dialog) were actually intended for the stage (cf. Raby, II, pp. 54–55).

their conversation is that Galathea is somewhat inclined to cooperate.

After this the go–between falsely reports to Pamphilus that his lady is going to be married. The lover is overwhelmed with despair. But the old woman reacts with words of reproach and suggests that the impending marriage may still be undone. Of concern to her is whether he intends to make good on the promise of payment. Assured again of eventual remuneration, she returns to the business at hand and persuades Galathea, now also tormented by love, to come to her house. Hardly have the two arrived, however, when Pamphilus bursts in and proceeds to force the beloved —in the absence of the go–between who slips out the door— to yield to his passion. Later, upon the return of the go–between, Galathea gives vent to bitterness over the outrage done to her. But the old woman denies complicity, and among the final verses of the poem tells the two they should get married.

As is evident, the author of the *Pamphilus* was by no means a slavish imitator of Ovid: his elegiac comedy shows a good deal of originality when it comes to the plot. Nonetheless, the influence of the Roman poet is extensive. Taking a brief look, for example, at vocabulary and expression, we notice that *Pamphilus* verse 415 which runs like this:

Non leve vulnus habent violenta Cupidinis arma,

(The fierce bolts of Cupid inflict a serious wound.)

seems to represent a fudging of *Ex ponto* I, 7, 50 and *Metamorphoses* IX, 543. Likewise verse 561 which goes as follows:

Quis nisi mentis inops sua semina mandat arene,

(Who, except an idiot, scatters seed on sand,)

probably corresponds to a combination of *Ars* I, 465 and *Heroides* V, 115. And for a borrowing taken strictly from the *Ars* we might compare *Pamphilus* 74:

Vix erit e mille, que neget una tibi

(There is hardly one woman in a thousand who will turn you down)

with verse 344 in Book One of the Roman poem:[24]

Vix erit e multis quæ neget una tibi.

The carryover is just short of verbatim. Here as elsewhere the imitator took care to avoid a total plagiarism.[25]

With respect to amatory precepts, one notices the dependency of parts of Venus' ars amandi on the Ars of the Roman poet. The lover is instructed, for example, to ingratiate himself with the servants of his lady (that they might influence the latter in his favor), and to achieve his ultimate goal by means of physical compulsion, two authentically Ovidian pieces of advice. All in all we might describe the love goddess' ars amandi as a compact, ad hoc version of the Ars. [26]

The works of Ovid were not the only source for the Pamphilus. Towards the end of her advice Venus advises the lover to make use of a go–between:

Et placeat vobis interpres semper utrisque,
    qui caute referat hoc, quod uterque cupit.
                                    (135–38)

(The two of you should always have a go–between, somebody

---

[24] All references to the Ars amatoria correspond to the version printed by J. H. Mozley. The English translations are also his (included in the same publication on pages opposite the original).

[25] See also Pamphilus 509 and 532 along with Amores II, 18, 9 and Heroides IV, 18 respectively. Some of the cited correspondences are drawn from Wilfried Blumenthal's study, "Untersuchungen zur Komödie "Pamphilus." See pp. 225–27.

[26] Ad hoc in that Venus' advice is adjusted so as to correspond to the particular circumstance of the protagonist.

who can do a shrewd job telling each one what he or she wants
[to hear].)

We might be tempted to associate this precept with Ovid's advice
concerning the use of the lady's handmaid as an intermediary:

> Sed prius ancillam captandæ nosse puellæ
>   Cura sit: accessus molliet tuos.
> Proxima consiliis dominæ sit ut illa, videto,
>   Neve parum tacitis conscia fida iocis.
> Hanc tu pollicitis, hanc tu corrumpe rogando:
>   Quod petis, ex facili, si volet illa, feres.
>   (*Ars* I, 351–56)

(But take care first to know the handmaid of the woman you
would win; she will make your approach easy. See that she be
nearest the counsels of her mistress, and the one who may be
trusted with the secret of your stolen sport. Corrupt her with
promises, corrupt her with prayers; if she be willing you will
gain your end with ease.)

More likely, however, is that the *Pamphilus* advice is part of an
adaptation deriving from another elegiac comedy, the *De nuntio
sagaci*. In both compositions we have:

1. A go–between acting on behalf of a seducer.
2. A reluctant but not disinterested ladylove.
3. An attempt by the go–between to persuade the ladylove to set
   aside her fears.
4. A temporary departure of the go–between after he (she) has
   delivered the ladylove to the seducer.
5. A subsequent pretense by the go–between to be unaware of what
   happened during his (her) absence.
6. A rejection of the ladylove's complaint by the go–between.
7. Advice by the go–between to the ladylove to avoid attributing
   importance to the seduction.

The similarity is too great to be fortuitous. Only one question remains: can we be sure that the *Pamphilus* is based on the *De nuntio sagaci*, not the *De nuntio sagaci* on the *Pamphilus*? The answer would have to be affirmative: whereas the *Pamphilus* was composed at or sometime after the middle of the eleven hundreds, the *De nuntio sagaci* dates in all likelihood from the first half of the same century.[27]

There is little need, therefore, to trace the intervention of the go–between as such to Ovid. But is it still possible, as some have maintained, that the type of the *Pamphilus* go–between (amoral old woman) represents an adaptation of the personage of Dipsas in the *Amores* of the Roman poet? Though a derivation cannot be ruled out entirely, some problems are involved. Dipsas —this should be stressed— is not a go–between: her mission is to advise the lady-love how to exploit male admirers, and her roll in the poem as a whole is minor (the only reference to her occurs in Book I, Chapter 8). On balance, then, one would do equally well, if not better, to consider the type of the intermediary in the *Pamphilus* as the author's personal contribution to ideas borrowed from the *De nuntio sagaci*.

The *Pamphilus* enjoyed immense popularity during the last three centuries of the Middle Ages.[28] The number alone of surviving manuscripts (some 60 complete copies are known to exist) attests to its appeal. In due season the poem even became an object of study in the Latin classroom, a result in part of the sententious character of its verse. The dubious moral tone seems to have mattered little. When in her final speech the intermediary says to the lover and his lady:

Hec tua sit coniux, vir sit et iste tuus! (v. 778)

(She should be your wife [said to Pamphilus], he should be your husband [said to Galathea].)

---

[27] Details concerning the dates of the two compositions can be had in Blumenthal, pp. 274–75.

[28] For a brief survey of its influence on vernacular literature in general see the introduction to the English translation of Thomas Garbaty.

she utters a sentiment well calculated to palliate all that went before.

At times the *Pamphilus* was attributed to Ovid and at times to Pamphilus the protagonist (the authorship of anonymous narratives was often assigned to one of the personæ), and sometimes to both Ovid and Pamphilus.[29] When a given copy of the poem circulated under the name of Ovid —nothing unusual in this— it simply came to form part of a notable mass of falsely attributed pieces which one may refer to in the aggregate as "pseudo–Ovidiana."[30]

These compositions were often diverse in nature, but in general their themes —or simply their meter— were of a sort as to allow them to be taken for authentic productions of the Roman poet. Thus, the *De somnio*, a piece found in a 13th century manuscript, was ascribed to Ovid because, it would seem, the content is reminiscent of *Amores* III, 5 (chapter relates a nocturnal dream). Likewise another piece beginning with the words "Rebus in humanis" was apparently added to a group of poems considered Ovidian simply because the topic has a bearing on sexuality.[31]

But of special interest here is the so called *Pseudo–Ars amatoria* (mid or late 12th century?), a brief guide to seduction in the form of precepts which circulated far and wide under the name of Ovid.[32] That the author knew and made use of the authentic *Ars* is repeatedly evident among the 95 distichs comprising the poem. With respect to expression, for example, we notice that verse 21 which runs:

---

[29] A double attribution could result from the poem being ascribed to the protagonist Pamphilus in the heading and then to Ovid by force of inclusion in a manuscript containing poems assigned to the Roman poet (whether authentic or not). For an example see Becker, pp. 13–4.

[30] The best general treatment of Pseudo–Ovidian literature remains that of Paul Lehmann in his *Pseudo–Antike Literatur des Mittelalters*, pp. 2–15.

[31] The text of both the *De somnio* and the "Rebus in humanis" can be had in Lehmann, pp. 63–5, and 88–9 respectively.

[32] A critical edition and study of the poem was published by Erich Thiel in *Mittellateinisches Jahrbuch*, V, 1968, pp. 115–80. All references given here correspond to his edition.

Providus imprimis oculis sibi querat amandam,

(First of all, he [the lover] should search carefully for a woman to love.)

is probably an adaptation of *Ars* I, 44:

Quærenda est oculis apta puella tuis.

And *Pseudo–Ars* 30 which goes as follows:

quove puella manet, recia tendat ibi.

(where the young woman tarries, there he should spread his nets.)

corresponds to all lights to *Ars* I, 45:

Scit bene venator cervis ubi retia tendat.

And *Pseudo–Ars* 69–70 which asserts:

Ferrea congeries dirumpitur improbitate
    et durum lapidem gutta cadendo cavat.

(An iron bulk is wreaked by impure ingredients and a hard rock is bored through by the dripping of water.)

is clearly a modified version of *Ars* I, 473 and 476:

Ferreus adsiduo consumitur anulus usu,
......
Dura tamen molli saxa cavantur aqua.

Likewise there is a certain sequence of precepts in the medieval poem similar to that in the *Ars*. In both compositions the lover is advised to look for a suitable ladylove, to attend and amuse her, to be persistent (in the assurance that her resistance will be temporary), to give a gift, and to make use of physical force at the appropriate moment.

The authentic *Ars* is not the only work to which the *Pseudo–Ars* shows a relationship: A clear and indisputable similarity to aspects of the *Pamphilus* is also in evidence. Analogous ideas are as follows:

1. In the *Pseudo–Ars* the lover is advised to get a go-between referred to in type as a clever talker and a woman. In the *Pamphilus* the lover is also advised to get a go–between albeit the only particular indicated at this point is that the person chosen should be a clever talker. In the sequel, however, it is a woman who assumes the task.
2. In the *Pseudo–Ars* the lover is instructed to remunerate the go between; but rather than render payment he should limit himself to a promise. An analogous development occurs in the course of the *Pamphilus*: the lover proposes to reward the go–between, but this intention eventually becomes suspect.
3. In the *Pseudo–Ars* the lover is told that the go–between should pursue the lady and incite her with sexual love (examples are given of what she might say). In the *Pamphilus* this is precisely what the go–between does.
4. In the *Pseudo–Ars* the lover is told that the go–between should use a pretext to manœuver the lady into a secure place (where she will be vulnerable to his sexual advances). In the *Pamphilus* this, again, is what the go–between does.

The parallel is too close to be accidental. And there is more: the advice concerning the need for a go–between goes as follows in the *Pseudo–Ars*:

> Nunccia queratur, in qua confidat uterque,
>   que narret caute, quicquid utrique placet. (39–40)

(A go–between should be sought, a woman in whom each can confide. She should be a shrewd talker, saying what is pleasing to both.)

and as follows in the *Pamphilus*:

> Et placeat vobis interpres semper utrisque,
>   qui caute referat hoc, quod uterque cupit. (135–36)

> (The two of you should always have a go–between, someone
> who can do a shrewd job telling each one what he or she wants
> [to hear].)

In this lead statement concerning the intermediary a relationship
both of sense and expression is evident. It seems that one of the two
poets knew the verses of the other and knew them directly.

Which poet, however, has yet to be determined. Neither work
refers explicitly to the other, and with one possible —but inconclusive— exception the similarities themselves give no clue to
chronological precedence.[33] Likewise the dates of composition are
too uncertain to be of use. The most one can say is that the
Pamphilus was probably composed in the middle of the 12th
century or not long thereafter, while the *Pseudo–Ars* may be equally
as old. And yet the dependency of the one on the other remains
incontestable: if the *Pamphilus* came first, then the *Pseudo–Ars* can
be regarded as a conversion of the elegiac comedy into precepts; if
the *Pseudo–Ars* came first, then much of the *Pamphilus* can be
regarded as a conversion of precepts into dramatic dialog.

In general imitative Ovidiana consists of poetry, especially
pseudo–Ovidiana which perforce would be in verse. The well known
De amore of Andreas Capellanus constitutes an exception. This
extensive treatise in prose which probably appeared in the 1180s
represents —or purports to represent— a scholastic analysis of
sexual love. But the debt to Ovid's poetry is evident. One notices,
for example, that the first two sections or Books (there are three in

---

[33] 33 In the *Pamphilus* the go–between is well delineated as an
unscrupulous elderly woman. In the *Pseudo–Ars* the go–between is
nondescript except for being characterized in one distich as capable of clever
talk and a woman ("nunccia"). But no reason for the gender preference is
given. Did the author of the *Pseudo–Ars* have the *Pamphilus* in mind as he
composed?

all) are analogous to the first two Books of the *Ars* in that they convey ideas relative to how love can be gained and then preserved. The third Book is analogous to the *Remedia amoris* in that it takes the opposite tack and conveys a negative posture towards love. On the other hand the treatise contains nothing corresponding to Book Three of the *Ars*, or advice to the ladies on how to make the most of masculine attention. The absence is consequential: the *De amore* is addressed to a man (by implication to every man) and hence advice to the opposite gender would be out of place.[34]

Andreas also laced his work here and there with Ovidian motifs and sentiments. In the Foreword, for instance, we find the neophyte lover referred to as a soldier ("new recruit of Love": cf. *Ars* I, 36), and the pursuit of love compared to a hunt for game ("this kind of hunting": cf. *Ars* I, 145).[35] In Book One we find the idea that jealousy is naturally concomitant with true love (."... love cannot exist without jealousy, ...": cf. *Ars* II, 443), and in Book Two the idea that love, once achieved, must be kept clandestine ("The man who wants to keep his love affair for a long time untroubled should above all things be careful not to let it be known to any outsider, but should keep it hidden from everybody, ...": cf. *Ars* II, 602–40).

In addition, Andreas had various medieval sources and among them was the *Pamphilus*, or possibly the *Pamphilus* and the *Pseudo–Ars* in conjunction. Thus in Chapter One of Book One he describes the (typical) lover as anxious about rumors ("He fears, too, that rumors of it may get abroad,..."), and as concerned with social class differences ("If he is a poor man, he also fears that the woman may scorn his poverty;").[36] But especially noteworthy in the same chapter is one of the observations concerning the usual effects of a deeply enamored state of mind:[37]

---

[34] The addressee (as stated in the preface) is a certain "Walter" who may be fictional.

[35] All excerpts from the *De amore* given in English are from the translation prepared by J. J. Parry (*The Art of Courtly Love*). All quotations from the original are from the edition of E. Trojel.

[36] 36 For an equivalent of these two quotations in the *Pamphilus* see vv. 255–56 and 49–52 respectively.

[37] As in Trojel, p. 6 (Parry, p. 29).

... statim enim adiutorium habere laborat et internuntium invenire.

(... straightway he [the lover] strives to get a helper and to find an intermediary.)

Many a modern reader of Andreas who is unfamiliar with the *Pamphilus* and the *Pseudo–Ars* might never have guessed that such could be a standard result of passionate love. But our author knew his audience, i.e., the clergy, and knew that they —or the well educated among them— would catch and appreciate the allusion.[38]

Most convincing of all, however, is a bit of literal borrowing from the *Pamphilus* which turns up in the dialog listed as G (an extensive part of the *De amore* consists of various types of model dialog between a would–be lover and his lady). Here at one point the woman is made to say in defense of her modesty:[39]

Nam, ut bene novistis, virgo cito perdit honorem, et eius fama modico rumore brevique dissolvitur aura.

(...for, as you know well, a maiden quickly loses her honor, and her reputation is ruined by a slight rumor and a little word.)

An assertion clearly adapted from *Pamphilus* vv. 413 and 417 where Galathea replies to the enticements of the go–between with:

Per Veneris morem virgo cito perdit honorem,

.....

Sepius immeritas incusat fama puellas,

---

[38] It should be stressed that the go–between is a figure typical of clerical amatory literature (cf. W. Creizenach, *Geschichte des neueren Dramas*, I, p. 41.) In the *De amore* mention of a go–between is infrequent. Yet it does exist. One wonders if Andreas himself had little interest in this sort of personage but felt obliged to make a concession to his readership.

[39] As in Trojel, p. 175 (Parry, p. 118.) The equivalence is drawn from Blumenthal (p. 283).

(A virgin soon loses her reputation by adhering to Venus ... Gossips often find fault with girls who are innocent.)[40]

Another facet of interest in the *De amore* is the radical divergence in sense between Books One and Two on the one hand and Book Three on the other. We have already seen that the difference in itself is not original, but derives from the contrast existing between the *Ars* of Ovid and his *Remedia amoris*. In the case of the Roman poet, however, mutual accord is not problematic: the reader encounters two opposite yet logically compatible approaches to sexual love: should someone choose to partake, then the *Ars* is his book; should someone choose to withdraw, then the *Remedia* is his book. As we are told in no uncertain terms near the start of the latter:[41]

> Siquis amat, quod amare juvat, feliciter ardet:
>   Gaudeat, et vento naviget ille suo.
> At siquis male fert indignæ regna puellæ,
>   Ne pereat, nostræ sentiat artis opem. (13–16)

(If any lover has delight in his love, blest is his passion: let him rejoice and sail on with favouring wind. But if any endures the tyranny of an unworthy mistress, lest he perish, let him learn the help my art can give.)

And soon after comes lengthy advice on how to break the bonds of love.

In the *De amore* the divergence assumes the character of outright inconsistency. We might, for example, consider a passage like this from Book One, Chapter Four:[42]

---

[40] Also worth comparison are the passages in the *De amore* and the *Pseudo–Ars* concerning the love of nuns and prostitutes (pp. 210–12 and 222 in the former, and vv. 3–10 in the latter).

[41] Quotation and translation given as in the version printed by J. H. Mozley (*The Remedies of Love*).

[42] As in Trojel, pp. 9–10 (Parry, p. 31).

Effectus autem amoris hic est, quia verus amator nulla posset avaritia offuscari, amor horridum et incultum omni facit formositate pollere, infimos natu etiam morum novit nobilitate ditare, superbos quoque solet humilitate beare, obsequia cunctis amorosus multa consvevit decenter parare. O, quam mira res est amor, qui tantis facit hominem fulgere virtutibus tantisque docet quemlibet bonis moribus abundare!

(Now it is the effect of love that a true lover cannot be degraded with any avarice. Love causes a rough and uncouth man to be distinguished for his handsomeness; it can endow a man even of the humblest birth with nobility of character; it blesses the proud with humility; and the man in love becomes accustomed to performing many services gracefully for everyone. O what a wonderful thing is love, which makes a man shine with so many virtues and teaches everyone, no matter who he is, so many good traits of character.)

And now a passage like the following from Book Three:[43]

Sed et alia ratio insidiari plurimum videtur amori. Quum enim ex amore mala cuncta sequantur, nullum penitus hominibus inde video procedere bonum, quia delectatio carnis, quæ inde multa aviditate suscipitur, non est genere boni, immo constat esse damnabile crimen, quæ etiam in coniugatos ipsis vix cum veniali culpa sine crimine toleratur, propheta testante qui ait: "Ecce enim [et] in iniquitatibus conceptus sum, et in peccatis concepit me mater mea."

(But still another argument seems very much opposed to love. Many evils come from love, but I do not see anything that is good for men comes from it; that delight of the flesh which we embrace with such great eagerness is not in the nature of a good, but rather, as men agree, it is a damnable sin which even in married persons is scarcely to be classed among the venial

---

[43] As in Trojel, p. 326 (Parry, pp. 193–94).

faults which are not sins, according to the word of the prophet, who said, "For behold I was conceived in iniquities and in sins did my mother conceive me.")

Can one possibly reconcile this pro and con aspect of the *De amore*? Though much has been written in an attempt to do so, nothing definitive has been established.[44] But perhaps such efforts are only in pursuit of a will–o'–the–wisp: Andreas himself may never have intended a continuous relationship to exist. Book Three is simply a contextually independent palinode, a development added to the first two books (the primary and essential development) for the purpose of deterring the intervention of a censor. We have seen the procedure repeatedly among the imitators of Ovid: the reader is presented with a sexually provocative statement and in conjunction a mitigating counterstatement. The only difference, then, in this regard between the *De amore* and, say, the *Pamphilus*, is that the palliative is more extensive in the former. It may be that the size of Books One and Two and the categorical pretense with which dissolute ideas are set forth called for a lengthy categorical undoing.

Nonetheless, of all the principal medieval Ovidiana, the *De amore* enjoys the distinction of having been publicly denounced by a church official. In a proclamation of 1277 the Archbishop of Paris declared the treatise reprobate (along with some other unspecified works) and in a joint decree condemned 219 diverse propositions dealing with philosophy and morality.

The Archbishop's decree represents an attempt by authorities to suppress Averroist philosophy, i.e., an interpretation of Aristotle which —among other singular notions— allows for truth on both sides of contradictory assertions. But is it possible to ascribe this outlook to Andreas? Nowhere does he refer to Averroist sources and not a single one of the 219 condemned propositions can be said to derive unequivocally from the *De amore*.[45] More likely, therefore,

---

[44] For an overview of the principal interpretations of the dichotomy see P. Allen, *The Art of Love: Amatory Fiction from Ovid to the Romance of the Rose*, p. 71.

[45] Such is the judgement of a specialist, Felix Schloesser. See his *Andreas Capellanus, seine Minnelehre und das christliche Weltbild um 1200*, pp.

is that the treatise simply happened to circulate among Averroist faculty and students at the University of Paris in the 1270s and was included in the condemnation on the basis of guilt by association.[46]

In any case nothing seems to have changed: the *De amore* continued to be read and copied; it was even translated a number of times into the vernacular. All with apparent impunity. One is inclined to believe that humor, not gravity, was the usual reaction of medieval readers. There is evidence: in the preface to a version done in French (late 13th century) the translator, a certain Drouart la Vache, reveals that when he first read the book he laughed so hard he was compelled by friends to compose a translation.[47] His merriment may well have been what Andreas expected.

Sometime near the middle of the 13th century there appeared the longest (more than 2,350 hexameters) and most audacious of our pseudo–Ovidiana, the *De vetula*.[48] According to a preface written by an alleged Byzantine official, the poem was composed by Ovid during his exile and buried with him at his death. But the preface is a sham: in the course of the three sections or Books which comprise the work one encounters a potpourri of themes marked by a distinctly medieval point of view, including: commentary on the social order, observations on sexuality, an amatory episode, discourse on philosophic and scientific topics, even a disquisition on astrology. The author was well rounded for his times and made a

---

369–71. The present writer is unaware of any effective attempt to gainsay this conclusion.

[46] Noteworthy is that Andreas tried to rationalize the transition from Book Two to Book Three. At the beginning of the latter he maintains he wrote in order that Walter might learn about love and then refrain; the result will be an increase in heavenly favor: "For God is more pleased with a man who is able to sin and does not, than with a man who has no opportunity to sin." Nothing here of Averroist double truth.

[47] For the text of Drouart see the edition of R. Bossuat, *Li Livres d'amours*, The reason for composing the translation corresponds to vv. 47–57.

[48] All references to the *De vetula* relate to the edition of Paul Klopsch (*Pseudo–Ovidius De Vetula*).

point of showing it.[49]

Binding the three sections together is an autobiographic pretense in which "Ovid" recounts why he changed from a life of worldliness and philandering to a life of sexual restraint and intellectual pursuit. Statements relative to this personal history can be found throughout the work, but the principal development occurs in the amatory episode (related in Book Two; the social and intellectual topics are dominant in Books One and Three). Of this central event extended discussion will be had later in Chapter Five. For the moment suffice it to say that an affinity to the *Pamphilus* is at once evident. Indeed, not only is the poet's audience treated to an obvious adaptation of the elegiac comedy, but an adaptation so employed as to constitute a unifying context for the diversity of subordinate topics. The pretended Ovid sought to make his book as attractive as possible: if the reader was partial to a social statement or an intellectual development there was something for him; if the reader was partial to the *Pamphilus* or *Pamphilus* type literature, there was something for him too. The procedure is not unique: an analogous structure and thematic accumulation turn up in the Archpriest's *Libro de buen amor*.

By the second half of the 13th century the *ætas Ovidiana* had come to an end.[50] The curriculum in most academic institutions was devoid of the classics and given over to subject matters considered more modern such as logic and philosophy. Not to say the study of antique literature had ceased altogether: there were still scholars here and there who were acquainted with the poetry of the Augustan Age. A good example can be had in the author of the *De vetula* himself.[51] But such men were unusual and probably did their reading outside the classroom or after the end of their formal education.

---

[49] For a long time the poem was attributed to a Frenchman, Richard de Fournival (active mid-13th century). But Klopsch, after a lengthy treatment of authorship (pp. 78–99), concludes that the attribution is improbable.

[50] For the demise of the classics after the 12th cent. see Paetow, p. 16ff.

[51] For examples of his familiarity with the classics see almost any page of footnote commentary in Klopsch's edition of the poem.

On the other hand, Latin study in itself remained firmly entrenched in the preparatory schools. A knowledge of the language, the academic lingua franca of the age, was still indispensable for a church career or admission to higher education. What, then, did a typical student of the 13th and 14th centuries read in conjunction with his grammar lesson? The answer is literature written for the most part during the medieval period. Excerpts from the *Vulgate* and various ecclesiastical writers were favorites along with a number of propædeutic compositions including the *faceti* or versified guides to proper etiquette, animal fables with an epigram, and the *Disticha* of Pseudo–Cato, a popular corpus vile since time immemorial. In addition, use was made, as we have seen, of the *Pamphilus*. The *Ars* had given way to an imitation.[52]

This neglect of the classics during the last few centuries of the Middle Ages is not without a bearing on the *Libro de buen amor*. The Archpriest wrote his masterpiece in the first half of the 14th century (more or less midway in the period when ancient writers ceased to be studied). Nonetheless, he refers to Ovid several times by name and cites him as a source author. Also, an extensive portion of the *Libro* contains amatory notions showing a distant similarity to those found in the *Ars*. Can it be, therefore, that our poet was directly familiar with the antique work in spite of the kind of academic training he most likely underwent?

A viable answer would have to take into account a comparison of the *Libro* with various pieces of medieval Ovidiana. There can be no doubt that the Archpriest made use of such literature: the role played by the *Pamphilus* in the creation of the *Libro* has long been known. But did the Spanish poet draw as well from other imitative compositions? In the pages to come we shall see that he probably did. In one instance, that of the *Pseudo–Ars*, the borrowing is certain and direct. In several other cases, that of the *De amore* and

---

[52] In one limited way access to the classics did continue to exist. If the literature of Antiquity had become a closed book in the classroom, it was still possible to find fragments of a given work in a florilegium or any medieval writing containing quotations from ancient authors (see, for example, the *Ars versificatoria* of Matthew of Vendôme). One might even speak of a fund of "quotables" passed on from one generation to another.

the *De vetula*, the borrowing —influence may be a better word— was apparently indirect and hence less tangible. The similarities, however, are to strong to be ignored.

The presence of medieval Ovidiana extends then for the length of the *Libro* (both in the overall thematic structure and in the affinity of many of the amatory adventures to the *Pamphilus*). One may justly state, for that matter, that if our Archpriest of Hita drew upon authentic Ovidian poetry for his Spanish poem, he has allowed that borrowing to be swamped by borrowing from imitative works. Indeed, the presence of antique Ovidiana —assuming it exists at all— is meager.

But to draw conclusions at this point would be premature. Let us turn instead to the business of tracing the Ovidian roots of the *Libro*. We might begin with a look at the poem in the light of the *De amore*.

II
De Amore

FELIX LECOY ONCE POINTED out that some of the ideas in the *Libro de buen amor* are so similar to ideas in the *De amore* of Andreas Capellanus as to suggest the Archpriest was familiar with the 12th century treatise.[1] The Spanish poet asserts, for example, in his prose preface that he wrote about the deception involved in "loco amor" so that people with sound reasoning would be able to make the right choice; even persons whose reasoning is warped will want, if nothing else, to avoid the bad reputation that stems from wickedness. But the poet adds —much to the surprise of his first time reader— that sinning is only human and if some persons should wish to make use of "loco amor" they will find in the *Libro* some pertinent instruction:[2]

> Empero, porque es umanal cosa el pecar, si algunos, lo que non les consejo, quisieren usar del loco amor, aquí fallarán algunas maneras para ello.

Andreas has something analogous to say: in Book One, Chapter Seven, of the *De amore* he tells his reader that if a clergyman commits the sins of the flesh he deserves to be deprived of the special nobility given him by God, i.e., his status as a cleric. Nonetheless Andreas goes on to propound that virtually no one is

---

[1] Felix Lecoy, *Recherches sur le* Libro de buen amor, pp. 290–91.

[2] The quoted prose passage appears on p. 79 in Corominas' edition of the *Libro*. Unless otherwise indicated all references to the Spanish poem correspond to this edition (see below n. 13).

without this sort of sin, and if a cleric should wish to indulge himself —the clergy above all are so inclined— he ought to conduct himself in a manner corresponding to his class background and the appropriate instruction contained in the *De amore.* The passage runs as follows:[3]

> Quia vix tamen unquam aliquis sine carnis crimine vivit, et clericorum sit vita propter otia multa continua et ciborum abundantiam copiosam præ aliis hominibus universis naturaliter corporis tentationi supposita, si aliquis clericus amoris voluerit subire certamina, iuxta sui sanguinis ordinem sive gradum, sicut superius edocet plenarie de gradibus hominum insinuata doctrina, suo sermone utatur et amoris studeat applicari militiæ.

> (But since hardly anyone ever lives without carnal sin, and since the life of the clergy is, because of the continual idleness and the great abundance of food, naturally more liable to temptations of the body than that of any other men, if any clerk should wish to enter into the lists of Love let him speak and apply himself to Love's service in accordance with the rank or standing of his parents, as we have already explained in regard to the different ranks of men.)

Lecoy has little else to say about a possible relationship between the *Libro* and the *De amore.* There are, however, various other analogous passages in the two compositions. We might take a look at a few. In one case the Archpriest speaks of the universal drive to seek a sexual union (sts. 71–3). It is, as he maintains, part of the natural order for both man and beast (but especially for man):

> Como dize Aristótiles,   cosa es verdadera,
> el mundo por dos cosas   trabaja: la primera,
> por aver mantenencia;   la otra cosa era
> por aver juntamiento   con fembra plazentera.

---

[3] Given as in the edition of Trojel, p. 221 (English version as in the translation of Parry, p. 142).

Si lo dexiés de mío   sería de culpar;
dizlo grand filósofo,   non só yo de reptar:
de lo que diz el sabio   non devemos dubdar,
ca por obra se prueva   el sabio e su fablar;

si diz verdad el sabio   claramente se prueva:
omne, aves, animalias,   toda bestia de cueva,
quieren segund natura   compaña siempre nueva,
e quánto más el omne   que a toda cosa s' mueva;

Andreas says largely the same thing when he informs his readers that love is inescapable; all human beings are subject to this compulsion regardless of differences in personal type or family background. His words are these:[4]

Cognosco igitur manifeste quod amor non consvevit homines discretionis stilo discernere, sed omnes pariter angit in suo, id est, amoris exercitu militare, non excipiens formam, non genus, neque sexum neque sanguinis inæqualitatem distinguens, sed hoc solum discernens, an aliquis sit aptus ad amoris arma ferenda.

(I know well that Love is not in the habit of differentiating men with titles of distinction, but that he obliges all equally to serve in his (that is, Love's) army, making no exceptions for beauty or birth and making no distinctions of sex or of inequality of family, considering only this, whether anybody is fit to bear Love's armor.)

And then there is this which the Archpriest has to say about the personal effects of love:

el amor faz sotil   al omne que es rudo,
fazle fablar fermoso   al que antes es mudo;

---

[4] As in Trojel, p. 37 (Parry, p. 45). The passage is part of a model conversation between a would–be lover and his lady.

> al omne que es covarde   fazlo muy atrevudo,
> al perezoso faz   ser presto e agudo,
>
> al mancebo mantiene   mucho en mancebez,
> e al viejo perder   faz mucho la vejez;
> faz blanco e fermoso   del negro como pez,
> lo que una nuez non val   amor le da gran prez. (156–57)

Andreas too has something to say about the ennobling effect of love:[5]

> Effectus autem amoris hic est, quia verus amator nulla posset avaritia offuscari, amor horridum et incultum omni facit formositate pollere, infimos natu etiam morum novit nobilitate ditare, superbos quoque solet humilitate beare, obsequia cunctis amorosus multa consvevit decenter parare. O, quam mira res est amor, qui tantis facit hominem fulgere virtutibus tantisque docet quemlibet bonis moribus abundare.

> (Now it is the effect of love that a true lover cannot be degraded with any avarice. Love causes a rough and uncouth man to be distinguished for his handsomeness; it can endow a man even of the humblest birth with nobility of character; it blesses the proud with humility; and the man in love becomes accustomed to performing many services gracefully for everyone. O what a wonderful thing is love, which makes a man shine with so many virtues and teaches everyone, no matter who he is, so many good traits of character!)

But the two writers also include in their respective compositions a contra development in the matter of love (sts. 181–422 in the *Libro*; the third section or Book Three in the *De amore*). And here too, in this antilove component we come across certain ideas in

---

[5] As in Trojel, pp. 9–10 (Parry, p. 31). We have seen this excerpt before in connection with Andreas' prolove–antilove dichotomy. The passage is worth repeating since it appears to be the one most similar to a *Libro* passage.

common. At one point, for example, the Archpriest states that love has a debilitating effect on the body (the poet is addressing himself to don Amor, the god of love):

> De cómo enflaqueces   las gentes e las dañas,
> muchos libros ay desto,   de cómo las engañas.
> con tus muchos doñeos   e con tus malas mañas
> siempre tiras la fuerça,   dízenlo en fazañas: (188)

The same notion turns up in Andreas; we read as follows:[6]

Nam ex amore et Veneris opere corpora deblitantur humana, et ideo homines efficiuntur in bello minus potentes. Debilitantur homines ex amore triplici satis rationabili causa; nam ex ipso Veneris opere, ut phyicalis monstrat auctoritas, corporis plurimum potentia minoratur, sed propter amorem corpus minoris cibi et potus assumptione nutritur, et ideo non immerito debet esse potentiæ brevioris. Præterea tollit amor etiam somnum et omni solet hominem privare quiete.

(By love and the work of Venus men's bodies are weakened, and so they are made less powerful in warfare. By love men are weakened in three very logical ways: by the mere act of Venus, as the physiologists tell us, the powers of the body are very much lessened; love causes one to eat less and drink less; and so not unreasonably the body, being less nourished, has less strength; finally, love takes away a man's sleep and deprives him of all rest.)

But for the Archpriest love is more than just physically debilitating; it is a cause of general indolence. In stanza 317 he makes the following reproach to the love god, don Amor:

> De la acidia eres   mesonero e posada,
> nunca quieres que omne   de bondad faga nada;

---

[6] As in Trojel, pp. 335–36 (Parry, pp. 198–99).

> desque lo ves baldío   dasle vida penada;
> en pecado comiença   e en tristeza acaba.

Andreas likewise sees this fault as a derivative of love:[7]

> Ad hæc: Amator quilibet ad omnia tardus reperitur et piger,
> nisi sint talia quæ ad usum pertinere videantur amoris. Negotia
> namque amorosus sua nec ullius curat amici, nec, si aliquis ei
> de quocunque facto loquatur, ipsius dictis intentas adhibet
> aures, nec precantis solet ad plenum verba percipere, nisi aliquid
> de suo referendo loquatur amore.

> (Besides this, we find that any lover is slow and lazy about
> everything except what may seem to be of service to his love. A
> man in love pays no attention to his own affairs or to those of
> any of his friends, and if anybody talks to him about something
> he has done he will not lend an attentive ear to what the man
> is saying, nor will he really hear the words of a suppliant unless
> the latter says something that has to do with his love.)

And for the sake of a final similarity one notices that both the
Archpriest and Andreas refer to love as a diabolic deception leading
to pain and death. The Spanish poet puts it this way:

> Manera as de diablo: adoquier que tú mores
> fazes temblar los omnes,   demudar las colores,
> perder seso e fabla,   sentir muchos dolores:
> trayes los omnes ciegos   que oyen tus loores; (405)

> A bretador semejas   quando tañe su brete:
> canta dulze con engaño,   al ave pone abeite
> fasta que le echa el lazo   quando el pie dentro mete:
> assegurando matas;   ¡quítate de mí, vete! (406)

Andreas, for his part, speaks as follows (by force of context the

---

[7] As in Trojel, pp. 327–28 (Parry, p. 194).

deceit in question relates to sexual love):[8]

> Nam eodem modo diabolus suis militibus et post eum ire
> volentibus dulcia proponit atque suavia et eos quodam modo
> reddit de impunitate ac longa vita securos, postmodum præmio
> sui ducatus accepto, id est peccatorum eis ære firmiter obligatis,
> ad insidiarum eos loca deducit, id est ad mortem, ubi dæmonum
> hostiles hominibus insidiæ præparantur, et eos in hostium
> derelinquit insidiis et cum hostibus spolia partitur et prædam,
> quia ipsos suæ fraudis ingeniis ad Tartara et [cum] dæmonum
> potestatem deductos cum aliis Tartareis potestatibus statutis
> pœnis affligit.

(In this way the Devil offers sweet and pleasant things to his
soldiers and to those who want to follow after him, and
somehow he makes them confident that they will have immu-
nity from punishment and will enjoy a long life; then, after he
has taken pay for his guidance —that is, when they are firmly
bound to him by the sinner's coin— he leads them to a place of
ambush —that is, to death— where the hostile snares of the
demons are laid for mankind. There he leaves them in the toils
of the enemy, and with this enemy he divides the spoils and the
booty; because after he has led them by his frauds and tricks
into hell and the power of the demons, then with the other
powers of hell he afflicts them by the torments he hands out to
them.)

Isolated passages like the foregoing are not the only similarity
between the *Libro* and the *De amore:* there is also a broad thematic
correspondence. The *De amore* amounts, as a whole, to an *ars
amandi* in conjunction with a second development critical of love
(where the antilove statements occur). Much the same may be said
for a part of the *Libro*: if we begin with stanza 181 and continue on
to stanza 422 we have an antilove development, and if we continue
on from 423 to 575 we have an *ars amandi* (followed by something

---

[8] As in Trojel, pp. 329–30 (Parry, pp. 195–96).

of a rerun in 607d to 648). There is, of course, a discrepancy in that the *ars amandi* does not precede, but follows the antilove development. The change, however, could have been required by the plot of the Spanish poem (assuming, for the moment, that our poet made direct use of the Latin treatise).

On the face of it, then, the similarities between the *De amore* and portions of the *Libro* are such as to suggest a direct dependency. And yet, upon further inspection, some problems turn up. First off, ideas in the *Libro* which appear to be adapted from the *De amore* are only approximately equivalent in sense. When the Archpriest, for example, speaks of his poem as affording instruction in sinful love he is addressing himself to an audience which included lay persons.[9] Andreas, however, in the analogous passage of the *De amore* is addressing himself strictly to clergymen. Likewise, when the Archpriest speaks of sexual desire as irresistible he refers to a variety of creatures and cites Aristotle in support. Andreas on the other hand limits his comments to human beings and cites neither Aristotle nor anyone else.

But even where there is similarity of sense one notices a lack of similarity of expression. The difference is not without importance: those parts of the *Libro* known to be based on a given source frequently show a likeness to that source both in idea and in the manner of expressing the idea. Thus a comparison of the "Endrina Adventure" (575–891) with the model text, the *Pamphilus*, reveals a good deal of correspondence in these two respects. A forthright example can be had in stanza 610 (the passage forms part of the *ars amandi* recited by Venus to the lovelorn protagonist). We read as follows:

> A toda mujer que mucho   otea o es risueña
> dil sin miedo tus deseos,   non te embargue vergüenza;
> apena que de mill una   te lo niegue; más desdeña:
> aunque la muger calle   en ello piensa e sueña.

---

[9] For evidence see sts. 161ff where the poet speaks to the women in his audience. In the medieval church clergy status was entirely a male preserve. No females —not even nuns— were ever considered to have the empowerment of clerics.

while in the *Pamphilus* counterpart we read:

> Et monstrare tuos animos nulli verearis,
> Vix erit e mille, que neget una tibi. (vv. 73–4)

(Do not hesitate to demonstrate your feelings; there is hardly one woman in a thousand who will turn you down.)

The Spanish version is more elaborate but conveys nonetheless the full import of the source passage. Much of verses *b* and *c*, for that matter, comes close to a translation.

For the sake of another example from the same episode we might look at stanza 629:

> Do fablares con ella,   si vieres que ay lugar,
> poquillo, como a miedo,   non dexes de jugar;
> muchas vezes cobdicia   lo que te va negar:
> darte ha lo que non cuidas   si non te das vagar;

The corresponding verses in the *Pamphilus* are 109–10:

> Si locus est, illi iocundis viribus insta!
>   Quod vix sperasti, mox dabit ipsa tibi.

(If the circumstance is suitable, be insistent in a playful but forceful way. What you hardly hoped for, she herself will presently give you.)

The same approach; it is in fact typical: again and again our poet introduces a degree of personal elaboration, but also takes care to include everything —or almost everything— conveyed by the model. In this respect much of the "Endrina" may rightly be described as a puffed up translation (*amplificatio*) of the *Pamphilus*.[10]

---

[10] Not to say that the Archpriest always adheres rigorously to the source: he often omits things, or adds things, or simply makes changes. But when he follows the sense of the original he usually does so closely.

Can one say the same for the Archpriest's use of the *De amore*? It seems out of the question: not a single correspondence is as strong as those between the "Endrina" and the *Pamphilus*. And this lesser accord goes hand in hand with another deficiency: little in the way of a similar sequence among related ideas: if our poet has borrowed amatory notions from the Latin treatise he has done so on a helter–skelter basis. Thus we see that *Libro* stanzas 71–73 relate to a *De amore* passage which appears on page 37 (Chapter One) of Trojel's edition. But *Libro* 156–57 relate to a *De amore* passage which appears farther back on pages 9–10. Likewise, *Libro* 188 in the Archpriest's development against love relates to a passage on pages 335–36 (Chapter Three) in the *De amore*. But *Libro* 317 in the poet's same contra theme relates to a passage on pages 327–29 of the *De amore*. Various other examples could be cited.[11]

And finally, it should be pointed out that our poet makes no attempt to identify his source. There are times, as we know, when he does not refer by name to a model text. But there are times when he does. In the case of the "Endrina," for example, we are told with respect to the origin of the story:

> Si villanía he dicho   aya y de vos perdón,
> que lo feo de la estoria   dize Pánfilo e Nasón. (891cd)

Or, as he makes clear in one of his excerpts from Pseudo–Cato:[12]

> Catón, sabio romano,   en su libro lo manda:
> diz que la poridat   en buen amigo anda; (568cd)

In view of the preceding considerations what is one to make of a possible direct dependency of the *Libro* on the *De amore* ? A just evaluation would have to take into account the following factors: if

---

[11] It might be added that many of the similar passages in support of love appear prior to stanza 181 in an autobiographic confession, not an *ars amandi*.

[12] The *Libro* passage corresponds to Book II, couplet 22, of the *Disticha* which can be found in *Minor Latin Poets* (ed. J. W. Duff and A. M. Duff), p. 608.

the Archpriest drew firsthand from Andreas' treatise for amatory ideas then he:

1. Made use of such ideas on a random basis.
2. Adapted the ideas so as to render the sense only partially similar to what exists in the original (contrary to his procedure elsewhere with a known source text).
3. Avoided reproducing the manner of expression found in the original (contrary to his procedure elsewhere with a known source text).
4. Did not acknowledge the provenance of his borrowing (contrary to his procedure here and there with other source texts).

We cannot of course reject outright the possibility that our poet had read the *De amore*. But on balance hard evidence that he did seems lacking. If there are similar ideas in the two works, the similarity is such as to indicate that he had only indirect knowledge of the Latin treatise. Or perhaps none at all: we could say just as well that the similarity is merely a consequence of both authors having drawn upon mutual source writings.[13]

Nonetheless, among the apparent similarities between the *De amore* and the *Libro* one is of true significance: the juxtaposition of extensive prolove and antilove statements with little concern for the resulting inconsistency.[14] To be sure, even in this regard we need

---

[13] For possible source versions of a given *Libro* passage one might consult the various critical editions of the poem (see Bibliography for a list of the best known). Corominas' edition, though sometimes criticized for tendentiousness in the matter of prosody, remains by far the richest with respect to insight and useful commentary.

[14] In the *Libro* the prolove development begins with the love god setting aside the accusations of the Archpriest as if they were only an emotional reaction to prior failures at love. A transition like this within dramatic dialog (as we have it in the *Libro*) is more effective than the pretense to a learned disquisition offered to the reader in the *De amore*. And yet, is it really possible to reconcile an accusation such as, say, the one in 184cd ("fazes a muchos omnes tanto se atrever/en ti, fasta que el cuerpo e el alma van perder.") with a guide to seduction?

not think the Archpriest composed in direct imitation of the *De amore:* there are other antecedents in imitative Ovidian literature.[15] But whatever the source, the upshot is a spiritual affinity: of importance for Andreas and our poet is not that the two statements be logically compatible, but that an antilove development be somewhere in place. The inclusion was apparently de rigueur: if in an *ars amandi* one caused the love god, don Amor, to make an affirmation like that in *Libro* 525 (part of a summons to importune a potential mistress with sexual invitations),

> Por una vez al día   que omne gelo pida,
> cient vegadas, de noche,   de amor es requerida:
> doña Venus jelo pide   por él toda su vida,
> en lo que l' mucho piden   anda muy encendida.

then one did well to have said something elsewhere to the effect that advice from Amor is unsound and sinful. And so, for example, we read in stanza 398:

> El que más a ti cree   anda más por mal cabo:
> a ellos e a ellas   a todos das mal ramo
> de pecado dañoso: de ál non te alabo;
> tristeza e flaqueza,   ál de ti non recabdo;

Stanza 398 and its context relate to the debilitating effect of love. But the immediate relevance matters little: what counted was that advice given by Amor be set down as destructive. And so it goes: there is hardly a verse in the *Libro* in promotion of sexual promiscuity which is not impugned in one sense or another by a notion set forth within stanzas 181–422. Our poet took care to defend his creation.

On the other hand if Andreas' "cover" is simply a collection of

---

[15] A good example can be had in the *Pseudo–Ars* in conjunction with another piece one might entitle the *Pseudo–Remedia amoris* (the two often circulated as an ensemble). For the text of the latter see Tiel, pp. 177–80. But any instance of a sexually promiscuous theme accompanied by an abrupt or incongruous palliative could have served as a catalyst.

moralistic (and misogynist) banalities, that of our Spanish author is not without artistic value.[16] Here occur the *exemplum* of the "Garçon que quería casar con tres mujeres" (189–96), and animal fables like "Las ranas en como demandavan Rey a don Júpiter" (199–206), and "Del cavallo e del asno" (237–45). Here also are such lines as "De mí sal qui m' mató e me tiró la vida" (272d), and "más orgullo e más brío tienes que toda España;" (304b: a rebuke made to don Amor). And here as well is the notable stanza 402:

> De la loçana fazes   muy necia e muy boba;
> fazes con tu gran fuego   como faze la loba:
> ¿al más fermoso lobo   o al enatío ajoba?
> a 'quél da de la mano,   e de aquél se encoba;

In itself the idea is a European commonplace. But in stanza 402 we have it expressed with anthropomorphic ingeniousness. An equivalent statement —or one we might take as such— in the antilove development of Andreas goes as follows:[17]

Luxuriosa est etiam omnis femina mundi, quia mulier quæ-

---

[16] At least to some extent. Unfortunately, the usual verve of the poet seems lacking in the theological diatribes proper. In particular, one might consider sts. 218–25abc which are among the least successful in the *Libro* (cf. Lecoy, p. 187). But Andreas, for his part, pulls all the stops. For an example of the extreme to which he carries his misogyny one might give thought to the following passage on feminine drunkenness (as in Parry, p. 207: the English alone will suffice): "Again, every woman is a drunkard, that is, she likes to drink wine. There is no woman who would blush to drink excellent Falernian with a hundred gossips in one day, nor will she be so refreshed by that many drinks of undiluted wine that she will refuse another if it is brought her. Wine that is turned she considers a great enemy, and a drink of water usually makes her sick. But if she finds a good wine with no water in it, she would rather lose a great deal of her property than forgo drinking her fill of that; therefore there is no woman who is not often subject to the sin of drunkenness." Doubtless, Andreas is being ironic. One would be hard put, however, to find assertions as preposterous as these in the *Libro*. Our Castilian poet had better sense and better taste.

[17] Cited as in Trojel, pp. 353–54 (Parry, p. 208).

libet, quantumcunque sit dignitatis honore præclara, si aliquem, licet vilissimum et abiectum, noverit in Veneris opere potentem, illum a suo concubito non repellit, nec est aliquis in opere Veneris potens, qui etiam cuiusvis mulieris posset quomodolibet mitigare libidinem.

(Every woman in the world is likewise wanton, because no woman, no matter how famous and honored she is, will refuse her embraces to any man, even the most vile and abject, if she knows that he is good at the work of Venus; yet there is no man so good at the work that he can satisfy the desires of any woman you please in any way at all.)

A time worn notion expressed in a formal prose. The distance between Andreas' version and that of the Archpriest is patent. All in all, then, it would probably be in order to set aside the contention that our poet made direct use of the *De amore* for amatory ideas in the *Libro*. The only important similarity —once again— is that both works contain a juxtaposing of an extensive pro and anti development. But that is an affinity which need not imply a strict derivation of the one from the other.

There are, however, other imitations of Ovid which the Archpriest clearly knew and drew upon. To wit: the *Pseudo–Ars* and the *Pamphilus*. Let us continue, therefore, by turning to these two poems and their corresponding episodes in the *Libro*. The *Pseudo–Ars* along with the *ars amandi* of don Amor, the god of love, (sts. 423–575) will be first.

III
Pseudo–Ars Amatoria

IT HAS LONG BEEN A commonplace to assume that the Archpriest was familiar with the *Ars amatoria* of Ovid and incorporated ideas from the Latin work into the *Libro*. Not everyone, to be sure, has agreed. Julio Cejador y Frauca, for example, who published an edition of the Spanish masterpiece early in the present century, maintained that the poet's apparent use of Ovid amounted to nothing more than a use of the *Pamphilus*.[1] But in general the current has been in the other direction. For evidence one need only consult the commentary of recent editors of the *Libro* such as Alberto Blecua and G. B. Gybbon–Monypenny.[2]

Cejador's opinion was, however, by no means farfetched. That the Archpriest made use of the *Pamphilus* as a model for one particular *Libro* episode, the seduction of the widow Endrina (sts. 576–891), can readily be demonstrated. In addition, the majority of the *Libro* passages one might possibly link to Ovid —other than those in the "Endrina" adventure— appear within a context analogous to an episode in the *Pamphilus*: an *ars amandi* recited by a love deity. One could have reason, therefore, at least initially, to believe that the elegiac comedy served as a model for most, if not all, of the Spanish poet's Ovidian development.

But a problem turns up: the *Pamphilus* appears to have no sure equivalent for many of the Ovidian type ideas in the *Libro*. Stanza 515, for instance, in which the lover is enjoined to make an

---

[1] Arcipreste de Hita, *Libro de buen amor*, ed. Julio Cejador y Frauca (cf. esp. I, xxvii and pp. 162–63).

[2] See esp. p. 112 in the edition of Blecua and p. 48 in that of Gybbon–Monypenny.

impression on his lady by singing in her presence clearly represents Ovidian advice but lacks a correspondence in the *Pamphilus*.[3] Inadequacy of this sort is so extensive as to reduce the direct role played by the elegiac comedy in the formation of the *Libro* to the "Endrina" and a few passages elsewhere.

It would be in order, therefore, to turn to the *Ars* as an alternative source for the Archpriest's Ovidian inspired verse. And indeed, Ovid's poem proves more viable in that it contains numerous ideas one could possibly construe as a *Libro* correspondence. One might even describe —albeit arbitrarily— various *Ars* type precepts as contributing to a thematic progression in a particular *Libro* episode.

But once again there is a problem. If at first sight it appears that Ovid's poem has a good number of passages corresponding to Ovidian type statements in the Spanish poem, upon careful consideration it becomes evident that most of the correspondence is faulty. More precisely: *Libro* passages thought to derive from the *Ars* usually differ so much in sense and spirit from the supposed Latin equivalents as to render a direct dependency doubtful.

And still another problem turns up: a lack of hard evidence that the *Ars* was known in the Iberian Peninsula prior to the 15th century. One could maintain, of course, that the presence of Ovidian amatory ideas in the *Libro* proves the Archpriest had managed to read the *Ars*. But this conclusion would be tenable only if it were certain that Ovidian ideas in the *Libro* were borrowed directly from Ovid. Is there sufficient evidence to justify the certainty? If not, then the probable unavailability of the *Ars* in 14th century Spain should properly strengthen the suspicion that our Castilian poet was not familiar with the poem.

And yet many commentators have continued to adhere to the *Ars* as a source for the Archpriest's Ovidian development. The final and decisive cause for doing so seems to be a matter of default: on the one hand there is the distant and problematic affinity of some of the *Libro* to the Latin work, and on the other hand the apparent absence of an alternative: if Ovid's poem on love was not the model text, what then was?

---

[3] For Ovid on singing see *Ars*, I, v. 595.

It may be time, however, for reconsideration. There is reason to believe that a viable substitute for the *Ars* does exist in the corpus of medieval Ovidiana, the *Pseudo–Ars amatoria*. In the pages to come we shall see how this brief imitative work offers an advantage over the original *Ars* as a source text for the Spanish poet's Ovidian development. Even more: the *Pseudo–Ars* contributes in a way to source unity: just as the pseudo–Ovidian *Pamphilus* was the direct model text for the "Endrina" episode (and several other stanzas), so this second pseudo–Ovidian composition was the direct model text for the rest of the Ovidian type statements in the Archpriest's poem.

But before demonstrating the suitability of the *Pseudo–Ars* as a source for the *Libro*, it would be well, for the sake of certainty, to take full stock of the inadequacy of the *Ars*. An appropriate procedure would be to examine closely the arguments of the two critics who have been the principal advocates of a *Libro–Ars* dependency.

The first one chronologically is Rudolph Schevill who in 1913 published a study containing a chapter on the Ovidian background of the *Libro*.[4] This American scholar drew up an extensive catalog of similar ideas, i.e., ideas he thought similar, drawn from the Spanish poem and several works of Ovid —but chiefly from the *Ars* — in order to demonstrate a dependency of the one work on the others. In fairness, one might add that he also tried in a small way to establish a structural similarity between the *Ars* and a part of the *Libro*. But it remains evident that the principal support for the Ovidian dependency is the sheer bulk of his catalog of similar ideas (more than 35).

Nonetheless, the reader with a strong knowledge of both the *Libro* and the *Ars* will hesitate: as previously indicated, possible correspondences between the two poems tend to be faulty. To get an idea of the shortcoming we might examine a few of the passages compared by Schevill.[5] At one point in the *Ars*, for example, the

---

[4] Rudolph Schevill, *Ovid and the Renascence in Spain.* The relationship of the *Libro* to Ovid is dealt with in Chapter Two (pp. 28–54).

[5] Consideration of Schevill's comparisons will be restricted to those involving the *Ars* which represent by far the greater part. The comparisons to other Ovidian poems are so arbitrary as to be insignificant. One might

Roman poet speaks of creatures in general as subject to a need for sexual union:

> Ales habet, quod amet; cum quo sua gaudia iungat,
>   Invenit in media femina piscis aqua;
> Cerva parem sequitur, serpens serpente tenetur,
>   Hæret adulterio cum cane nexa canis;
> Læta salitur ovis: tauro quoque læta iuvenca est:
>   Sustinet inmundum sima capella marem;
> In furias agitantur equæ, spatioque remota
>   Per loca dividuos amne sequuntur equos. (Ars II, 481–88)

(The bird has one he may love; in mid–sea the female fish finds one with whom to unite in pleasure; the hind follows her mate, serpent is clasped by serpent, the hound is joined in clinging lechery to the bitch; gladly the ewe endures the leap, the heifer rejoices in the bull, the snub–nosed goat supports her unclean lord; mares are excited to frenzy, and through regions far removed follow the stallions, though streams divide them.)

Schevill relates this passage from the *Ars* to *Libro* stanza 73 in which the Spanish poet speaks of the constant search by man and beast for a new (sexual) partner:[6]

> si diz verdat el sabio   claramente se prueva:
> omne, aves, animalias,   toda bestia de cueva,
> quieren segund natura   compaña siempre nueva,
> e quánto más el omne   que a toda cosa s'mueva;

Likewise the two poets, as Schevill points out, have something to say about the salutary effect of love. Ovid represents sensual

---

consider, for example, Schevill's (p. 43) association of vv. 413–16 in the *Remedia amoris* with *Libro* st. 274. The shared idea (fatigue and malaise after copulation) is in no wise peculiar to Ovid.

   [6] As already indicated, *Libro* quotations are, in general, from the edition of Corominas. Schevill who published his study in 1913 quoted, of course, from elsewhere.

pleasure as softening the spirit of the primeval brute:

Tum genus humanum solis errabat in agris,
Idque meræ vires et rude corpus erat;
Silva domus fuerat, cibus herba, cubilia frondes:
Iamque diu nulli cognitus alter erat.
Blanda truces animos fertur mollisse voluptas. (II, 473–77)

(Then mankind wandered in the lonely fields; brute strength was theirs and forms uncouth; woodland was their home, their food grass, their bedding leaves; and for long none knew his fellow. Beguiling pleasure is said to have softened those fierce spirits:)

Schevill equates this passage to *Libro* stanzas 156–57 where the Archpriest explains the ways in which love has a refining effect on the lover:

el amor faz sotil   al omne que es rudo,
fazle fablar fermoso   al que antes es mudo,
al omne que es covarde   fazlo muy atrevudo,
al perezoso faz   ser presto e agudo,

al mancebo mantiene   mucho en mancebez,
e al viejo perder   faz mucho la vejez;
faz blanco e fermoso   del negro como pez,
lo que una nuez non val   amor le da gran prez:

We have seen these *Libro* passages already in connection with the *De amore*. Does Ovid fare better than Andreas as the source author? The answer would seem to be no. First off, one notices that the *Libro–Ars* correspondences are characterized by widely differing motifs and expressions. Just as it was with the medieval treatise, so too is it with almost every comparison one can make with Ovid's guide to love. This divergence should not be disregarded: in those parts of the Spanish poem for which a direct source has been firmly established our poet expresses himself (at least on occasion) in a fashion highly similar to the model text.

But turning to the primary sense conveyed by each of the passages one notices that it must be arbitrarily modified in order to gain the correspondence. More precisely: if we interpret the passages in strict accord with their particular meaning and context, then the correspondences either shrink to very little, or —even worse— show a degree of conflict.

Thus, in the first of the comparisons reproduced from Schevill the sense of the *Libro* stanza (all creatures are driven by a sexual urge) is indeed roughly similar to the corresponding *Ars* passage.[7] A serious problem develops, however, if one takes into account the Archpriest's attribution of the idea to "el sabio." Looking back to the immediately preceding stanzas or 71 and 72 we see that by force of context the reference is to Aristotle, not to Ovid:

> Como dize Aristótiles,   cosa es verdadera,
> el mundo por dos cosas   trabaja: la primera,
> por aver mantenencia;   la otra cosa era
> por aver juntamiento   con fembra plazentera.
>
> Si lo dexiés de mío   sería de culpar;
> dizlo grand filósofo,   non só yo de reptar:
> de lo que diz el sabio   non devemos dubdar,
> ca por obra se prueva   el sabio e su fablar;

But Schevill is of another mind and suggests that "el sabio" could still be the Roman poet. As evidence, he mentions what he calls the Archpriest's "offhand manner of citing authorities" and points out that "Aristótiles," fits the metrical scheme in 71a, while "Ovidio" or "Nasón" (used elsewhere in the *Libro* to designate Ovid) do not.

Nonetheless, there can be little doubt that "el sabio" refers to the Greek philosopher since an idea more or less equivalent to that in stanzas 71 and 73 can be found among his works.[8] We need not

---

[7] Noteworthy is the thought in 73c ("quieren segund natura compaña siempre nueva,") which is peculiar to the Archpriest. It can provide an excuse for philandering.

[8] For ideas similar to these stanzas among the writings attributed to

of course conclude that the Archpriest had firsthand knowledge of the writings of the Stagirite. The source may have been an intermediate text such as, say, a florilegium; or something oral like a classroom lecture or even banter with colleagues. But one thing is certain: the ideas attributed to Aristotle are, in fact, Aristotelian. To suggest, therefore, that when the poet cites the Greek philosopher and reproduces some of his thought, he is, in reality, adapting from someone else, is wide of the mark.

In the second group of Schevill's comparisons the similarity proves upon investigation to be specious: the two poets are not talking about the same thing. Thus, when Ovid speaks of "beguiling pleasure" as mollifying ferocity (one should note that the Roman poet's "voluptas" and the Archpriest's "amor" do not necessarily coincide) he is speaking of the capacity of sexual desire to distract from an incentive to hostility. That such is the pertinent interpretation is evident from the wider context in which the reader is informed of the various ways by which a lover might manipulate sexuality in order to sooth a mistress infuriated by infidelity.

Libro stanzas 156–57, on the other hand, reflect a concept typical of "Courtly Love." As we know, in the medieval literature dealing with the theme (or constituent ideas) there was no universally accepted code of values. Nonetheless, certain notions tend to recur, among which is the belief that the condition itself of being enamored exerts a refining effect on the lover.[9] We would search in vain, however, for a statement to this effect in the *Ars* or any of the authentic works of Ovid. For the Augustan poet it is not love which leads to refinement, but refinement —to be had, for instance, by reading the *Ars*— which leads to love. And love itself is understood as a kind of game ("lusus") in which the sexes vie for a largely sensual satisfaction. The spirit of the *Ars* is foreign to the spirit of *Libro* stanzas 156–57.

As previously noted, Schevill sought to demonstrate something of a similarity of structure between the *Ars* and a part of the *Libro*.

Aristotle see the article of Erasmo Buceta, "La 'Política' de Aristóteles, fuente de unos versos del *Libro de buen amor*." The *Politics*, one might add, is not the only possible Aristotelian source.

[9] See Mott, p. 10 for an entry relative to "the ennobling effect of love."

We need not dwell on this aspect of his study since a later scholar treated the seeming possibility with greater thoroughness, and to him we shall shortly turn. Suffice it to say that the similarity as described by Schevill is vitiated by his failure to account for the many differences and even contradictions which exist in the one poem vis a vis the other and offset any parallel of thematic development. Again, Schevill's study, to the extent it has weight, is a collection of isolated excerpts offered as evidence that the Archpriest drew directly from Ovid.

A more precise study of the relationship of the *Libro* to the *Ars* can be found in Lecoy's *Recherches sur* le Libro de buen amor.[10] Like Schevill before him, this French scholar maintained that the Archpriest had borrowed directly from Ovid, and in support of the dependency put together —his principal evidence— a systematic table of 13 correspondences between the two poets.

All the pairings in the table refer to only one Ovidian work, the *Ars*, and to only one section of the *Libro*, stanzas 423–75, or the episode in which the love god, don Amor, delivers a lecture (an *ars amandi*) to the despondent protagonist, the Archpriest himself. For Lecoy to limit his Ovid–*Libro* correspondences in this way was appropriate. Whereas passages in the Spanish masterpiece thought to derive from other works of the Roman poet would comprise a scattering of heterogeneous snippets, the various pieces of amatory advice set forth by don Amor have one sure trait in common with the *Ars:* collectively they constitute an *ars amandi*. If there is, in short, any part of the *Libro* for which one could possibly make a convincing case for direct derivation from the poetry of Ovid it is stanzas 423–575.

And yet, problems persist. For one thing it is obvious that many of Lecoy's pairings, like those of Schevill, are not truly equivalent. As an example we might consider the precept concerning wine drinking or *Ars I*, 589–92 which the French scholar compares in his table to *Libro* 528–48.[11] The Latin passage says the following:

---

[10] The study in question appears on pp. 290–306.

[11] Quotations from the *Ars* adhere to the verse numeration in Mozley's version. The numbering cited by Lecoy differs slightly.

Certa tibi a nobis dabitur mensura bibendi:
Officium præstant mensque pedesque suum.
Iurgia præcipue vino stimulata caveto,
Et nimium faciles ad fera bella manus.

(I will give you a sure measure of drinking: let mind and feet perform their duty. Especially beware of quarrels caused by wine, and of hands too quick to brutal fight.)

The *Libro* passage in question is lengthy, but to get the gist we need reproduce no more than the introductory stanza:[12]

Buenas costumbres deves   en ti siempre aver.
Guárdate, sobre todo,   mucho vino bever,
que el vino fizo a Lot   con sus fijas bolver,
e en vergüeña del mundo,   en saña de Dios cær. (528)

Both poets counsel moderation in drinking. But one perceives that Ovid's position is a matter of pragmatism, while that of the Archpriest pertains to propriety. The difference proves considerable: it is not drunkenness in itself which the Roman poet regards as a fault (in *Ars* I, 229–44 he speaks favorably of wine as a stimulant for sexual passion), but the resultant incapacitation which could cause the lover to fail at an opportune moment. That such is the case is evident from *Ars* I, 597–600 (the passage is properly a part of the precept on wine drinking although Lecoy fails to include it in the corresponding entry) where Ovid suggests the lover pretend to be drunk: the feigned inebriation will allow him to take liberties which would otherwise not be tolerated:

Ebrietas ut vera nocet, sic ficta iuvabit:
Fac titubet blæso subdola lingua sono,
Ut, quicquid facias dicasve protervius æquo,

---

[12] The remaining stanzas or 529–48 contain the quasi autonomous *exemplum* of the drunken hermit and some elaboration on the idea set forth in 528ab.

Credatur nimium causa fuisse merum.

(As real drunkenness does harm, so will feigned bring profit: make your crafty tongue stumble in stammering talk, so that whatever you do or say more freely than you should, may be put down to too much wine.)

Can one possibly reconcile advice like this with don Amor's reason for opposing drink? In reality the Archpriest's approach to wine has little in common with that of Ovid.[13]

But setting aside for the moment the question of precept similarity one notices that another and particularly serious defect of Lecoy's correspondences is the sequential disaccord between entries from the *Libro* and entries from the *Ars*. More precisely: precepts in the don Amor lecture thought to be drawn from Book One of the Latin poem are intermixed with precepts from Book Two as if there were no distinction.[14] Instances of this lack of agreement are as follows: *Libro* 453 from *Ars* II (lover should be submissive to his lady); *Libro* 454–56 and 468–73 from *Ars* I (lover should avoid being unduly modest with his lady); *Libro* 474–84 from *Ars* II (lover should avoid neglecting his lady); *Libro* 488–89 from *Ars* II (lover should ingratiate himself with other persons associated with his lady); *Libro* 515 from *Ars* I (lover should entertain his lady with a virtuoso performance); *Libro* 527 from *Ars* I (lover should avoid sexual involvement with another woman having to do with his lady); *Libro* 528–48 from *Ars* I (lover should avoid excessive consumption of wine); *Libro* 564–65 from *Ars* II (lover should

---

[13] That the Spanish poet sought to "moralize" Ovid seems unlikely. In this regard one might consider *Libro* 564 (compared by Lecoy to *Ars* II, 372–408): "De una cosa te guarda quando amares alguna:/ non te sepa que amas otra mujer ninguna,/ si non, todo tu afán es sombra de la luna,/ e es como quien siembra en río o en laguna;."

[14] The reader will recall that the *Ars* is divided into three sections or "Books" according to topic. Book One gives advice to the lover on how to win the favors of a mistress; Book Two advice on how to maintain her favors; Book Three advice to the women on how to make the most of the lover's attentions. This last Book is irrelevant to the formation of the *Libro*.

conceal his infidelity).[15]

Lecoy has, however, an explanation for the disorder. Prior to presenting the table he writes (p. 295):[16]

> In Juan Ruiz the development does not reproduce the plan of Ovid. His precepts are not at all distributed into two categories in accordance with whether they apply to the conquest or to the preservation of the love affair. The Spanish poet limits himself to aligning a certain number of precepts such that it is hard to grasp clearly the idea which determined the order in which they are set up. On the other hand since he was more concerned with teaching how to gain the love of one's lady rather than how to preserve it —the Archpriest seems to have had a fickle disposition— the rules he formulates derive without distinction from either Book I of Ovid or Book II. And yet the didactic element has been carefully preserved. It is a veritable lesson which Love delivers to the poet, a veritable course which he expounds to him, and he (the love god) reproaches him for having thought it would be possible to gain his end without having previously undergone instruction.

The careful reader will wonder what purpose there is in simply affirming that a lesson is conveyed by the *Libro* precepts when what matters is an affirmation that the lesson conveyed is the *same* as

---

[15] It should be noted that the first four *Libro* precepts (not reproduced) as they are in Lecoy's table are in sequence vis a vis the *Ars*. Up to this point, then, there appears to be something of a structural agreement. Upon close inspection, however, it becomes evident that the similarity of structure is contrived. The second precept common to both *artes amandi* is a summons to the lover to make use of a third party (a woman) as a go–between (*Ars* I, 351–96; *Libro* sts. 436–43). But one notices that an integral aspect of the advice (lover should not become sexually involved with the go–between) does not appear in don Amor's lesson until stanza 527 and is therefore well out of sequence with respect to Ovid's poem.

[16] This passage (given in English for convenience sake) along with the table of correspondences constitutes the sine qua non in Lecoy's argumentation.

that of the Latin poem. Sound reasoning cannot be otherwise: if the structure of the don Amor lecture differs notably from that of the Latin poem and the lesson imparted differs as well, one may rightly conclude that the *Ars* was not the source —or not the direct source — for the Spanish composition.

One perceives, however, that Lecoy's table of correspondences serves not only to associate precepts, but also to imply that the instruction in love given by don Amor is more or less equivalent to the instruction given by Ovid. And herein lies the core weakness of Lecoy's procedure. At first sight the table does indeed appear to establish something of an equivalence. But presently, as one reads on in the *Recherches*, it becomes evident that the table was able to do so by failing to account properly, i.e., beforehand, for the many discrepancies which compromise the similarity of the one lesson in love to the other.[17] Put another way: if Lecoy had laid out from the start everything in the don Amor lecture at variance or in conflict with the *Ars*, the cogency of his table of correspondences would have diminished considerably.

We might take stock of the extent of this disaccord. One may summarize as follows:

1. Precepts in the don Amor lecture thought to derive from precepts in the *Ars* frequently show a notable divergence from the sense of the supposed model version. In addition, an equivalence of expression or motif is all but non–existent.
2. The sequential order of such precepts does not correspond.
3. There are precepts in the don Amor lecture not in the *Ars*.
4. There are precepts in the don Amor lecture which contradict

---

[17] Prior to the presentation of the correspondence table in the *Recherches* there is discussion of only one of the discrepancies, that of the differing sequence of precepts. The other discrepancies are not specified until after the appearance of the table and are spoken of —by way of conjecture— as changes purposefully introduced by the Archpriest. The cautious reader can only puzzle at procedure like this: given that the table is able to demonstrate a dependency of the one *ars amandi* on the other precisely because of what is omitted, is it permissible thereafter to evaluate the omissions in the light of the would–be dependency?

precepts in the *Ars*.

5. It can be shown that the *Pamphilus* played a role in the formation of don Amor's precepts. The presence of the 12th century
poem is more certain than the presence of the *Ars*.

6. In the course of the don Amor lecture the Spanish poet mentions
the name of Ovid several times, but nowhere is there an
indication that he considered him the author of the *Ars* (which
is never cited). On the other hand there can be little doubt that
he associated the Roman poet with the authorship of a pseudo–
Ovidian composition, the *Pamphilus*.

For the sake of clarity it would be well to take a cursory look at
the above forms of discrepancy. As we have already done so for
those numbered one and two we may pass directly to three and
continue on in sequence.[18]

Turning, then, to the precepts that figure in the *Libro* but not in
the *Ars*, let us give thought to 518abc in which don Amor speaks of
a particular method for making an impression on the lady-love:

> Prueva fer ligerezas   e fazer valentía:
> quier lo vea o non,   saberlo ha algún día;
> non será tan esquiva   que no ayas mejoría;

To impress the beloved the lover should put on a demonstration
of prowess. Lecoy discusses this precept and describes (p. 298) the
import as "more medieval" (than Ovidian). His judgement is sound
to the extent that an equivalent is not to be found in the *Ars*. But
the French scholar makes no attempt to determine a written source
for the idea. Rather, he implies that it represents the Spanish poet's
personal addition to a precept borrowed from Ovid (*Ars* I, 595–96:
advice to the lover to entertain his lady by singing in her presence).

And yet, the possibility of a source text should not be ruled out.
If, for example, one could come up with a 12th or 13th century *ars
amandi* containing equivalents for don Amor's Ovidian type advice

---

[18] But with a hiatus between four and five to allow for a comparison of
precepts in the *Pseudo–Ars* and the *Libro*.

along with a specific equivalent for the non–Ovidian idea in 518abc, then, by force of comprehensiveness, one would have a pre-existing text more suitable than the *Ars* as a source model for the don Amor lecture. As we shall see, the type of *ars amandi* referred to is not merely hypothetical: just such a combination exists in the *Pseudo–Ars*.

Another precept in the *Libro* without some form of correspon–dence in Ovid's poem and this time even in conflict with what the Roman poet has to say is that found in stanza 562:

> Ante otros de acerca   tú mucho non la cates,
> non le fagas señales: a ti mismo non mates;
> ca muchos lo entienden   que lo provaron antes;
> de lexos algarea quedo,   non te arrebates.

The lover, according to don Amor, should avoid expressing his sentiments to the lady while other people are nearby; he may, however, communicate discreetly from a distance.[19] Ovid, for his part, gives advice to the contrary. We read the following in Book One of the *Ars*:

> Nec tibi de mediis aliquot transire columnas
>   Sit pudor, aut lateri continuasse latus;
> Nec sine te curvo sedeat speciosa theatro:
>   Quod spectes, umeris adferet illa suis.
> Illam respicias, illam mirere licebit:
>   Multa supercilio, multa loquare notis.
> Et plaudas, aliquam mimo saltante puellam:
>   Et faveas illi, quisquis agatur amans.
> Cum surgit, surges; donec sedet illa, sedebis;
>   Arbitrio dominæ tempora perde tuæ. (495–504)

(Neither hesitate to slip past some of the columns that part you,

---

[19] The precept amounts to another notion typical of "Courtly Love" (cf. Mott, p. 12). The purpose, of course, is to avoid revealing the existence of the affaire.

nor to join your side to hers; nor let her sit in the round theatre, her fair looks by you unheeded: something worth looking at she will bring on her shoulders. On her you may turn your looks, her you may admire: much let your eyebrows, much let your gestures say. Applaud when an actor portrays some woman in his dance, and favor whoever be the lover that is played. When she rises you will rise; while she sits you will sit too; waste time at your mistress' will.)

As with *Libro* stanza 518, Lecoy describes the idea in stanza 562 as more medieval in outlook than Ovidian. And also as with 518 he has nothing to say about a possible source for the idea in 562 other than to imply that it probably derives from the Archpriest himself.

Nonetheless, we may make the same observation for stanza 562 as for 518: if one could produce a written source in the form of an *ars amandi* containing an equivalent for the generality of don Amor's Ovidian advice along with an equivalent for 562, then, all things being equal, one would have a preferable alternative to the *Ars* for the love god's lesson in love. And again, just such an alternative can be had in the *Pseudo–Ars*.

For verification we might look now at a comparison of similar ideas in the don Amor lecture and the pseudo–Ovidian composition. One notices the following correspondences:

1. If you want to love, you must first learn how:

> *LIBRO* 430abc:
> Si quieres amar dueña   o otra qualquier mujer,
> muchas cosas avrás   primero a deprender
> para que te ella quiera   en amor acoger.

> *PSEUDO–ARS* 1–2:
> Si quem forte iuvat subdi sapienter amori,
>   sic amet incipiens, ut mea musa docet.

(If anyone should want to engage in love the right way, then let him begin in accordance with the teaching of my verse.)

2. To start off, select the proper woman: look for one who has certain charms; stick more or less to your own social class:

> LIBRO 430d; 431:
> Sabe primeramente   la mujer escoger:
>
> Cata mujer fermosa,   donosa e loçana,
> que non sea muy luenga   ni otrossí enana;
> si podieres, non quieras   amar mujer villana,
> ca de amor non sabe: es como bausana;
>
> PSEUDO–ARS 21–22; 25–27:
> Providus imprimis oculis sibi querat amandam,
>   eligat ex multis, que placet una sibi.
>
> Sed virtutis opes, generacio, forma decora
>   ante repensetur, ne nimis alta petat.
> Diligat equalem vel paulo se meliorem,[20]

(First of all, he should search carefully for a woman to love. Let him select someone he likes from among the many.

Let him give thought above all to quality of character, type of family, and good looks. But he should not aim too high. Let him single out someone who is his social equal or only a little better than himself;)

3. Get a shrewd go–between:

> LIBRO 437abc:
> Puña, en quanto puedas,   que la tu mensajera
> sea bien razonada,   sotil e costumera:
> sepa mentir fermoso   e siga la carrera,

---

[20] Is it possible that *Libro* 431b renders into Castilian the sense of "ne nimis altam petat" (he should not seek someone who is too tall) instead of "ne nimis alta petat"? Ovid himself has nothing to say about the appropriate height of the ladylove.

PSEUDO–ARS 39–40:
Nunccia queratur, in qua confidat uterque,
    que narret caute, quicquid utrique placet.

(A go–between should be sought, a woman in whom each
can confide. She should be a shrewd talker, saying what is
pleasing to both.)

4. Give gifts. If not, then at least make promises of gifts; doing this
will incite her:

LIBRO 451:
De tus joyas fermosas   cada que dar podieres—
quando dar non quesieres   o quando non tovieres,
promete e manda mucho   maguer non gelo dieres:
luego estará afuziada,   fará lo que quesieres.

PSEUDO–ARS 41–42:[21]

---

[21] The recipient of the dubious gift–giving in *Pseudo–Ars* 41–42 is the
go–between, while the recipient in *Libro* 451, by force of context, is the
ladylove. But there is reason to believe that 451 originally occupied a locus
in reference to the go–between and subsequently lost that position through
scribal garbling. Looking at the surrounding stanzas one notices that 452 is
a duplicate of 611 in the Endrina episode and was probably not intended by
the poet to appear in this part of the *Libro* (where the sense is both abrupt
and redundant). Likewise, as Corominas (pp. 186–88) proposes, the series
436–43 (referring to the go–between) should be removed from the present
locus and reinserted after the series 444–51 (referring to the ladylove). The
Catalan scholar's transposition is quite appropriate although some scholars
have objected (for an instance see the article of Martín de Riquer, "Ordenación de estrofas en el *Libro de buen amor*"). I would propose, however, that
the transposition be modified in one small way: that 451 be shifted to the
position occupied by the intrusive 452 and a lacuna be supposed for the now
empty 451. Structured in this way 451 would follow immediately after
436–43 and refer by context to the go–between.

In support of the modification one might consider the following: 1) The
sense conveyed by 451, if understood as referring to the ladylove, is such as
to render superfluous the remainder of don Amor's lesson in love: if all the

Muneret hanc iuvenis, quod sit super hec studiosa,
et plus, quam tribuat, polliceatur ei.

(The young man should reward her so that she will go about
this matter eagerly. But rather than actually give something he
should only make make promises to her.)

5. Pursue your beloved; go where she is and there take action:

LIBRO 454abc:
Requiere a menudo   a la que bien quesieres
—non ayas miedo della—   quanto tiempo tovieres;
verigueña non te embargue   do con ella estodieres:

PSEUDO–ARS 29–30:
Inde locum querat, quo semper amica moretur,
   quove puella manet, recia tendat ibi.

(He should then seek out the place where his ladylove
always spends time; where the young woman tarries, there he
should spread his nets.)

6. Entertain your beloved: sing; amuse her in any way you can; put

---

lover has to do is make an empty promise of gifts and the beloved will react
such that "fará lo que quesieres" why need anything more be said? Indeed,
the lady can be had with ease and at no expense. 2) The sense of 451
understood, again, as relative to the ladylove, would be contradicted by
550cd farther down in don Amor's *ars amandi* where the lover is advised
with respect to his lady that: "de quanto que pudieres non le seas escasso,/
ni en lo que l'prometieres la trayas a traspasso." 3) If 451 is understood as
referring to the go–between, then the sense will be reinforced by 514ab
where the lover is told concerning his intermediary that: "si algo non le
dieres, cosa mucha o poca,/ sey franco de palabra, no l'digas razón loca:"
And to these considerations one might add that for the Archpriest to incite
his go–between with an offer of jewels would be eminently apropos: when
he eventually engages a woman to act as intermediary we learn of her that:
"Era vieja bohona de las que venden joyas:" (699a).

on a demonstration of prowess:

LIBRO 515–16; 518ab:

Si sabes estrumentes   bien tañer e templar,
si sabes e avienes   en fermoso cantar,
a las vegadas, poco,   en onesto lugar
do la mujer te oya,   non dexes de provar.

Si una cosa sola   a la mujer non muda,
muchas cosas juntadas   fazerte han ayuda;
desque lo oye la dueña   mucho en ello cúida:
non puede ser que a tiempo   a bien non te recuda.

Prueva fer ligerezas   e fazer valentía:
quier lo vea o non,   saberlo ha algún día;

PSEUDO-ARS 31–34:
Huc veniat ludens, cantet suspiria coram,
    que si non novit, militet arte sua.
Hic temptet vires, hic dulcia verba loquatur,
    quod placet, hoc faciat, res velud ipsa dabit.

(Here he should come in a light hearted mood; he should sing and sigh in her presence. If he is unable to do this he should resort to his imagination: he might put on a show of physical agility, or he might speak to her in gentle tones; whatever is pleasing, that he should do; something is sure to be effective.)

7. The lover should be persistent in his pursuit. If the lady is at first resistive she will presently burn with desire. Water can bore through a hard rock with constant dripping.

LIBRO 524ad:
A toda cosa brava   grand uso la amansa:
la dueña mucho brava   usando se faz mansa.

PSEUDO–ARS 53–54:
Forsitan in primis dabit aspera verba puella,
    sed cito, que prius est aspera, mollis erit.

(It may be that at first the young lady will have harsh words
to offer. But she who was harsh will soon be soft.)

LIBRO 525:
Por una vez al día   que omne gelo pida,
cient vegadas, de noche,   de amor es requerida:
doña Venus j[e]lo pide   por él toda su vida,
en lo que l'mucho piden   anda muy encendida.

PSEUDO–ARS: 63–64; 67–68:
Ach quociens teneram que nunquam novit amare,
    talibus ingeniis languidus urit amor.

Femina, quod prohibet, cupit et vult sepe rogari,
    improbitas vincit pectora, frangit amor.

(How many times, in fact, does it happen that a lukewarm
attraction, when skillfully provoked, causes a young girl without
experience to burn with passion.

What a woman does not permit she really desires; she wants to
be constantly begged; sexual desire will overcome her will to
resist; love will break it down.)

LIBRO 526:
Muy blanda es el agua   e da en piedra muy dura:
muchas vegadas dando   faze grand cavadura;
por grand uso el rudo   sabe grande letura;
mujer mucho seguida   olvida la cordura.

PSEUDO–ARS 69–72:
Ferrea congeries dirumpitur improbitate
    et durum lapidem gutta cadendo cavat.
Sic multis precibus et longo temporis usu

colloquium fieri sponte puella volet.

(An iron bulk is wrecked by impure ingredients, and a hard rock is bored through by the dripping of water. Thus it is that after a good deal of entreaty and the passing of time a young woman will freely agree to a conversation.)

8. Exercise restraint:

> *LIBRO* 553:
> En todos los tus fechos,   en fablar e en ál,
> escoge la mesura   e lo que es cumunal:
> como en todas cosas   poner mesura val,
> assí, sin la mesura,   todo parece mal.

> *PSEUDO–ARS* 147–48:
> Sed tamen in cunctis placidus modus est adhibendus,
>   nam sine mensura nil valet esse bonum.

(But in all these things a gentle moderation should be exercised since nothing is good that is done without restraint.)

9. When in the presence of your lady do not let other people perceive your affection. You may, however, communicate from a distance:

> *LIBRO* 562:
> Ante otros de acerca   tú mucho non la cates,
> non le fagas señales: a ti mismo non mates;
> ca muchos lo entienden   que lo provaron antes;
> de lexos algarea quedo,   non te arrebates.

> *PSEUDO–ARS* 177–78:
> Sepe superciliis vel nutu longius instet,
>   si prope non audet voce sonante loqui.

(He should always be ready to wink or nod from a distance, if it would be risky to speak aloud up close.)

10. Be quiet about your love affair; talking about it to others can cause harm:

> *LIBRO* 566–67:
> Sobre todas las cosas   fabla de su bondat.
> Non te alabes della,   ca es grand torpedat:
> muchos pierden la dueña   por dezir necedat;
> quequier que por ti faga   tenlo en poridat:
>
> si mucho te celares   mucho fará por ti;
> do fallé poridat   de grado compartí;
> de omne mesturero   nunca me entremetí
> a muchos, de las dueñas   por esto los partí;
>
> *PSEUDO–ARS* 187–90:
> Gaudia que sumpsit, curet celare modestus
>   nec nomen domine publicet ipse palam.
> Qui culpa propria placidam sibi perdit amicam,
>   perpetuo doleat rusticitate sua.

(The pleasure he has had he should modestly seek to conceal. He should not make known the name of his mistress in public. He who loses his dear ladylove through his own fault should perpetually grieve over his crudity.)

As can be seen, the similarity between the two lessons in love is often one of expression as well as of idea. One might consider in particular *Libro* 430ab and *Pseudo–Ars* 1–2; *Libro* 437ab and *Pseudo–Ars* 39–40 (note how "mensajera" reproduces exactly the sense of "nunccia"); *Libro* 454a and *Pseudo–Ars* 29; *Libro* 518a and *Pseudo–Ars* 33 (to "vires"); *Libro* 524ad and *Pseudo–Ars* 53–54; *Libro* 526 and *Pseudo–Ars* 70–72; *Libro* 553 and *Pseudo–Ars* 147–48 (the *Libro* stanza is virtually a translation of the *Pseudo–Ars* passage); *Libro* 562 and *Pseudo–Ars* 177–78; *Libro* 566d–67a and *Pseudo–Ars* 187. To establish a rapprochement as close as this between the *Libro* and the *Ars* of Ovid would be impossible.

Likewise, with the exception of the precepts relative to the go–between, there is agreement of sequential order between similar precepts in the one *ars amandi* and the other. The accord is particularly noteworthy in the case of the non–Ovidian advice we have seen previously or *Libro* stanzas 518ab and 562 and *Pseudo–Ars* 33 and 177–78 respectively. This analogousness alone would justify preferring the medieval imitative poem to Ovid's original as a model for don Amor's amatory advice.

And yet one notices that the *Pseudo–Ars* is deficient in one respect as a source for don Amor's lesson in love: a number of precepts one might possibly derive from the *Ars* have no equivalent in the pseudo–Ovidian poem. There are four such, including: (1) advice to the lover to ingratiate himself with other persons having to do with his lady (*Libro* 488–89); (2) advice to avoid becoming sexually involved with the go–between (*Libro* 527); (3) advice to avoid excessive use of wine (*Libro* 528–49a); (4) advice to conceal infidelity from the ladylove (*Libro* 564–65).[22]

---

[22] I omit as insubstantial three precepts which Lecoy distinguishes in don Amor's lesson and traces to the *Ars*. These include 1) Advice to the lover to be submissive to the ladylove (453); 2) Advice to be bold and use force with the ladylove (454–56; 468–69); 3) Advice to avoid absence from the ladylove (472–73). In the case of (1) the patently anti–Ovidian sentiment in verses ab of 453 (Gradécegelo mucho lo que por ti feziere:/póngelo en mayor precio de quanto ello valiere;) makes it little likely that the remaining two verses are based on Ovid. This stanza for that matter should properly refer by force of context to the go–between (as a result of Corominas' transposing of stanzas). In the case of (2) a summons to employ physical force to induce the beloved to submit would surely constitute an Ovidian link between don Amor's lesson and the *Ars* if the idea were common to both *artes amandi*. But the notion is not clearly present in the love god's advice —Lecoy appears to have "read it in"— and the remainder of the supposed correspondence is so vague as to be indeterminate. In the case of (3) there is a problem of context: Ovid's advice pertains to preserving the favors of a beloved who has already been seduced, while don Amor's advice concerns —to all lights— procedure in the conquest of a ladylove yet to be won (cf 473cd). We have seen that Lecoy explained such differences by maintaining that the Archpriest introduced a deliberate simplification of the *Ars* into the Spanish counterpart. It must be said, however, that a notable variation between two versions of a precept which in itself constitutes nothing more than common sense could just as well indicate that the one

We need not be surprised that some of the advice in the love
god's lesson should fail to appear in the *Pseudo–Ars* since there is
nothing in the Spanish composition to indicate that the poet
confined himself to a single source for his amatory notions. On the
contrary: it can be shown with virtual certainty that one of the four
Libro precepts lacking for an equivalent in the pseudo–Ovidian *ars
amandi* is an adaptation of a passage in the *Pamphilus*. The precept
is that contained in stanzas 488–89 (lover should ingratiate himself
with other people associated with his lady). We read as follows:

> Otrossí quando vieres   a quien usa con ella,
> quier sea suyo o non,   fáblal por amor della;
> si podieres, dal' algo: non le ayas querella,
> ca estas cosas pueden   a la mujer trælla.

> Por poquilla de cosa   del tu aver que l' dieres,
> servirte ha lealmente,   fará lo que quesieres;
> que poco o que mucho   dal' cada que podieres:
> fará por los dineros   todo quanto pedieres.

The two stanzas are listed in Lecoy's table as relating to *Ars* II,
251–60 where an analogous idea can be found (but one should note
that there is no similarity of expression and Ovid's precept refers
specifically to servants or slaves while the *Libro* counterpart is
open-ended):

> Nec pudor ancillas, ut quæque erit ordine prima,
>   Nec tibi sit servos demeruisse pudor.
> Nomine quemque suo (nulla est iactura) saluta,
>   Iunge tuis humiles, ambitiose manus.
> Sed tamen et servo (levis est impensa) roganti
>   Porrige Fortunæ munera parva die:
> Porrige et ancillæ, qua pœnas luce pependit
>   Lusa maritali Gallica veste manus.
> Fac plebem, mihi crede, tuam; sit semper in illa

---

version does not derive from the other.

Ianitor et thalami qui jacet ante fores.

(Blush not to win over handmaidens, as each stands first in rank, nor blush to win over slaves. Salute each one by name: you lose nothing thereby; clasp low–born hands, ambitious ones, in yours. Ay, even to a slave, should he ask you [the cost is trivial], offer some small gift on the day of Fortune; offer it to a handmaid also, on the day that the Gallic band paid penalty, tricked by the marriage–robe. Believe me, make the humble folk your own; let the gate keeper ever be one of them, and he who lies before her chamber door.)

On the other hand if we turn to the *Pamphilus* we find the following advice in the *ars amandi* recited by the goddess Venus to the would–be lover, Pamphilus (the lesson takes place under conditions analogous to those of the don Amor lecture, i.e., a lesson recited by a love deity to a frustrated protagonist):

> Et famulos famulasque domus sibi sepe loquentes
>   Allice colloquiis muneribusque tuis,
> Ut semper referant de te bona uerba uicissim
>   Et pascant dominam laudibus usque tuam! (vv. 125–28)

(And so with friendly conversation and the giving of gifts gain the confidence of her household servants, both the men and the women, especially those who often talk to her, so that they, each in turn, may always speak well of you. Have them "feed" your lady with your praises!)

As is evident the four verses from the *Pamphilus* show a certain similarity of expression as well as of idea to *Libro* stanzas 488–89. This factor in itself makes the *Pamphilus* a more likely source for the precept than the *Ars*. But that is not all: one can point to evidence elsewhere in the *Libro* in support of the association. Since the "Endrina episode", or stanzas 576–890 represents the Archpriest's version of the *Pamphilus* as a whole, we might expect to come upon a second rendering of these same four verses from the elegiac comedy. And we do: the corresponding locus is stanzas

638–39 where the following advice is given:

> Quando vieres algunos   de los de su compaña,
> fazles muchos plazeres,   fáblales bien con maña;
> quand' o[y]' esto la dueña   su coraçón se baña:
> servidor lisonjero   a su señor engaña;
>
> ado son muchos tizones   e muchos tizonadores,
> será el fuego mayor   e mayores los ardores;
> ado muchos le dixieren   tus bienes e tus loores,
> mayor será la su quexa   e sus deseos mayores;

A comparison of stanzas 638 and 488 shows that both are fairly similar (especially with respect to the first two verses) and give the gist of *Pamphilus* 128–29. But in the second stanza of each group, or 639 and 489, there is a partial difference. In 639 the Archpriest continues to develop his theme in accordance with the strict sense of the *Pamphilus* passage and describes the effect which the flattery of the intermediaries will have on the beloved. In 489, on the other hand, our poet modifies the sense of the *Pamphilus* passage by concentrating on the idea of gift giving mentioned in 488c. Such giving, we are told, is useful as a means for insuring loyalty and obedience. But at the same time the somewhat indefinite characterization of what is given ("algo" and "poquilla de cosa del tu aver"), becomes money in no uncertain terms ("dineros") as if that had been all along the specific nature of what the lover was to hand out. This swerve allows the poet to launch thereafter into a goliardic style tirade against the power of money (stanzas 490–513), a development of somewhat limited relevance to don Amor's *ars amandi* theme. It would seem that 488–89 is simply an adaptation of some *Pamphilus* verses utilized for the sake of introducing the antimoney theme contained in the next 24 stanzas.

Why should the Archpriest resort to the *Pamphilus* for an idea he would have found in the *Ars* if he had been using the latter as a model text? By now one might tend to conclude that Ovid's poem was not a direct model for don Amor's lesson in love and lay the matter to rest. But doing so at this point may still be hasty. Given that the precepts in the Spanish *ars amandi* derive from a number of sources, the possibility could exist that the *Ars* constituted one of those sources if only for a few pieces of advice. Of the four precepts listed above as having no equivalent in the *Pseudo–Ars* no more than stanzas 498–99 seem to stem from the *Pamphilus*. Can it be that the other three or those concerning wine drinking, sexual involvement with the go–between and the concealment of infidelity were adapted from the Roman poet's instruction in love?

We have seen that the attitude of the Archpriest towards wine does not truly coincide with that of Ovid. One may rightly harbor doubts, therefore, that the *Ars* was a source for the *Libro* precept. Nonetheless, when investigating poetry written in the tradition of *mester de clerecía* it would usually be better to point to some possible source model than to have no source at all. Considering, then, that both the *Pseudo–Ars* and the *Pamphilus* are silent on the matter of wine one might, perhaps, continue to suggest the *Ars* as a basis for what don Amor has to say about drink.

And yet there is no need to fall back on Ovid. In the case of the wine precept a suitable written source can be had in a non–Ovidian text which the Archpriest most certainly knew and drew upon, the *Disticha* of pseudo–Cato.[23] If we turn to the first section of this late antique, quasi medieval collection of maxims, we come across a series of prose sententiæ among which one will find the following:[24]

Vino tempera. (Be moderate with wine.)

And if we turn to the prolog to this part of the compilation we find a statement to the effect that the maxims were written to give instruction to those persons who have deviated from reputable conduct:

Cum animadverterem quam plurimos graviter in via morum errare, succurrendum opinioni eorum et consulendum famæ existimavi, maxime ut gloriose viverent et honorem continge-

---

[23] For the part played by the *Disticha* in the formation of the *Libro* see the article of Edwin J. Webber, "Juan Ruiz and Ovid."

[24] This and the following excerpt (including the translations) occur on pp. 592–93 and 594–95 in *Minor Latin Poets*.

rent. nunc te, fili karissime, docebo ...

(As I noticed the very great number of those who go
seriously astray in the path of conduct, I decided that I should
come to the aid of their belief and take thought for their
reputation, so that they might live with the utmost glory and
attain honour. Now I shall teach you dearest son ...)

All of which accords far better than the *Ars* with the reasons of the
Spanish poet for avoiding excess with wine. Though dependent
primarily on the *Pseudo–Ars*, Don Amor's precepts appear to derive
from a variety of sources.

But if some of the love god's advice has little to do with Ovid,
his admonition concerning a sexual relationship with the intermediary stands squarely in the Ovidian tradition. The precept in question
is succinct, taking up no more than one stanza. We read as follows:

> Guárdate non te abuelvas   a la casamentera:
> doñear non la quieras,   ca es una manera
> por que t' farié perder   a la entendedera:
> ca una conlueça de otra   siempre tiene dentera. (527)

Ovid, for his part, has this to say in an analogous vein:

> Quæris, an hanc ipsam prosit violare ministram?
>   Talibus admissis alea grandis inest.
> Hæc a concubitu fit sedula, tardior illa;
>   Hæc dominæ munus te parat, illa sibi.
> Casus in eventu est: licet hic indulgeat ausis,
>   Consilium tamen est abstinuisse meum. (*Ars*, I, 375–80)

(You will ask, whether it profits to seduce the maid herself;
such an enterprise involves much hazard. An intrigue makes one
more eager, another more sluggish; this one wins you for her
mistress, that one for herself. It may turn out well or ill; though
the issue favor the hazard, yet my counsel is abstain.)

At first sight there appears to be something of a correspondence between the two passages since the maid whom the Roman poet has in mind is also the woman he recommends for go–between service. As he had told his reader previously in verses 351–52:

> Sed prius ancillam captandæ nosse puellæ
> Cura sit: accessus molliet illa tuos.

(But take care first to know the handmaid of the woman you would win; she will make your approach easy.)

Nonetheless this same advice to use the maid as a go–between raises a problem for the *Libro*–Ars correspondence: don Amor has something quite different to say about the person of the intermediary:

> La mujer que embiares   de ti sea parienta
> que bien leal te sea;   non sea su servienta:
> non lo sepa la dueña   porque la otra non mienta;
> non pued ser, quien mal casa,   que non se arrepienta.
>   (st. 436)[25]
> .....
>
> Si parienta non tienes atal,   toma unas viejas
> que andan las iglesias   e saben las callejas:
> grandes cuentas al cuello,   saben muchas consejas;
> con lágrimas de Moisen   escantan las orejas; (st. 438)

The go–between should not be a servant of the ladylove; rather she should be a relative of the lover, or, failing that, a woman chosen from among certain old hags who frequent the churches and know their way around back alleys. The type of the Archpriest's intermediary is obviously not drawn from the *Ars*.

But in spite of the conflict one might still suppose that the

---

[25] The stanzas quoted appear in the edition of Corominas in the loci corresponding to numbers 444 and 446 respectively (as a result of his transposition of 436–43). But to avoid confusion the enumeration given here is the traditional one.

Libro version of the precept stems ultimately from Ovid: if the Archpriest prefers someone other than a servant as go–between, the fact that he suggests the use of an intermediary at all is an indication he has the *Ars* in mind. And such, in effect, is Lecoy's view of the origin of the *Libro* advice. As the French scholar would have it, the Castilian poet has updated the person of the Roman poet's go–between, converting her into a professional go–between, a figure typical of the social order in the late Middle Ages.

And yet a problem arises: if the Archpriest stipulates that the go–between be either a relative or an old hag why should he subsequently caution the lover not to have a sexual relationship with her? Lecoy explains this now peculiar admonition as follows: having modified the personage of the go–between, the Spanish poet returned to his Latin model and continued to draw upon authentic Ovidian advice even where doing so was no longer apropos. In the French scholar's own expression the advice to avoid sexual intimacy with the intermediary is a "survival" (p. 305).

Lecoy's argument puts a strain, however, on credibility. The several gratuitous assumptions involved would seem to "multiply entities beyond necessity." His procedure, for that matter, constitutes a forthright example of falling back on the *Ars* for want of another more viable source. But just such a possibility exists: the *De vetula*. As we shall see below in the corresponding chapter, several *Libro* problems relating to source origin —including the puzzle in stanza 527— can be plausibly resolved by turning to the pseudo–Ovidian poem as a model text. Additional discussion of 527 will therefore be put off to a later point. For the moment let it be enough to observe that the Archpriest could have more readily know the 12th century composition than the *Ars.*

The remaining precept in the *Libro* with a possible derivation from the *Ars* is the one dealing with the lover's need to conceal infidelities from his lady. It occurs in stanzas 564–65:

> De una cosa te guarda   quando amares alguna:
> non te sepa que amas   otra mujer ninguna,
> si non, todo tu afán   es sombra de la luna,
> e es como quien siembra   en río o en laguna;

piensa si consintrá tu cavallo tal freno
que tu entendedera amasse a Frey Moreno:
pues piensa por ti mesmo e cata bien tu seno,
e por tu coraçón juzgarás el ajeno.

As with the advice in stanzas 474–84 or the summons to the lover not to be excessively absent from his lady, in 564–65 we have a notion that is not so much Ovidian as rather a commonplace. But in one respect these stanzas seem to show the influence of the Roman poet: they appear close to the end of don Amor's lesson and in a context possibly implying that the sexual favors of the lady-love have already been won.[26] This accords with the position of the *Ars* counterpart which occurs in Book Two of the Latin poem (vv. 372–392), or the section dealing with the preservation of an established love affair. The sequential position of *Libro* 564–65 is therefore correct —grosso modo at least— and lends support to the possibility of the precept having been adapted directly from the Roman poet.

Nonetheless, any attempt to derive the idea in stanzas 564–65 from Ovid's poem will run into a problem of equivalence: the two poets do not attribute the same result to the lover's infidelity. According to the Archpriest, if the lady learns the lover is attracted to someone else, all his efforts will have been in vain, i.e., his love will be rejected. As he tells us in 564cd:

si non, todo tu afán es sombra de la luna,
e es como quien siembra en río o en laguna;

Such is not what we read in the *Ars*. The Roman poet first laments the jealous rage to which the lover will be subjected (*Ars* II,

---

[26] Several other stanzas, most notably 562 and 566 seem to suggest that the projected love affair in don Amor's *ars amandi* has reached a stage in which the lover is on intimate terms with his lady. This impression is reinforced by the use of "entendedera" in 565b. On the other hand if we understand the sense of "amares" in 564a as indicating that the lady has yet to be won, then the presence of a distinctively Ovidian element in 564–65 is reduced to nil.

373–408), and then continues with the following advice:

> Quæ bene celaris, siquæ tamen acta patebunt,
> Illa, licet pateant, tu tamen usque nega.
> Tum neque subiectus, solito nec blandior esto:
> Hæc animi multum signa nocentis habent:
> Sed lateri ne parce tuo: pax omnis in uno est;
> Concubitu prior est infitianda venus. (Ars II, 409–14)

(Should what you have well concealed be nevertheless made manifest, manifest though it be yet deny it ever. Be not submissive then, nor more flattering than of wont; such signs point overmuch to guilt; but spare no efforts; peace is centered in one thing: by caresses must the former passion be disproved.)

The assumption here would seem to be that if the lover is involved with a second mistress his passion for the first can be expected to diminish. The poet's advice, accordingly, is that the unfaithful lover continue to demonstrate sexual ardor with his outraged mistress while at the same time denying his guilt: in so doing he will prove his fidelity and ultimately bring about a reconciliation.[27] Whether the procedure always succeeds is, of course, open to question (one senses the presence of irony). But this much is certain: for Ovid the affair with the cheated mistress is by no means over. Indeed, he soon goes on to suggest the lover deliberately allow his lady to suspect some cheating:

> Fac timeat de te, tepidamque recalface mentem:
> Palleat indicio criminis illa tui;
> O quater et quotiens numero conprendere non est
> Felicem, de quo læsa puella dolet:
> Quæ, simul invitas crimen pervenit ad aures,
> Excidit, et miseræ voxque colorque fugit.
> Ille ego sim, cuius laniet furiosa capillos:

---

[27] In the verses following 414 Ovid recommends the disloyal lover make use of aphrodisiacs to insure the intensity of his passion.

Ille ego sim, teneras cui petat ungue genas,
Quem videat lacrimans, quem torvis spectet ocellis,
Quo sine non possit vivere, posse velit. (*Ars* II, 445–54)

(See that she has fears about you, and fire anew her cooling thoughts; let her grow pale at hearing of your guilt; O four times and unnumbered times happy is he over whom an injured woman grieves; who, as soon as the charge has reached her unwilling ears, faints away, and voice and color leave her unhappy frame. May I be he whose hair she furiously rends! may I be he whose tender cheeks her nails attack! whom weeping she regards, at whom she glares with angry eyes, without whom she could not live, though fain she would.)

By permitting the lady to have doubts about his loyalty the lover will provoke her jealously and thereby inject fresh passion into a cooling relationship. With machination like this we are clearly far from the sense of *Libro* stanzas 564–65. What Ovid has to say about infidelity has little to do with the simplistic advice of don Amor.

At this point we have covered enough ground to decide whether one can still maintain that the Archpriest made use of the *Ars* as a source text for the don Amor lecture. As we have seen, running the length of the Spanish *ars amandi* is a succession of precepts amounting to a lesson in seduction which corresponds more to the medieval *Pseudo–Ars* than to the *Ars* of Ovid. But in spite of this agreement there remain a number of amatory ideas in don Amor's lesson which have no equivalent in the imitative poem. Upon comparison, however, most of these additional ideas show less affinity to the *Ars* than to other sources possibly used by the poet for "bits and pieces." One instance in particular stands out: it can be shown with near certainty that an Ovidian type precept was carried over not from the *Ars* but from the pseudo–Ovidian *Pamphilus*. All in all, therefore, it would be safe to conclude that if our poet was familiar with a true work of Ovid, there is nothing of substance in don Amor's lesson to provide confirmation.[28]

---

[28] It should be added that Lecoy (p. 312) sees st. 612 in the *Pamphilus*

The entirety of the Archpriest's verses based on the *Pseudo–Ars* may be said to consist in precepts expressed in second person command form along with (in a few cases) a small amount of clarification. These adaptations from the pseudo–Ovidian poem turn up here and there over the length of don Amor's lecture on love. In themselves, however, they do not constitute an extensive amount of poetry. Of the 608 lines of verse comprising the episode something in the order of 55 may be said to represent a carry over from the imitative composition. And if to this latter figure we add the number of precept verses stemming from other sources, the overall total is not much greater. The amatory directives as such, then, represent only a modest portion of the love god's lesson in love.

But we might have expected as much: the reader of don Amor's lecture soon notices that a good part of the episode consists of illustrative or explanatory elaborations built into the context of certain precepts. These illustrations have their origin in a variety of sources and —significantly— are not all totally relevant to don Amor's *ars amandi*. For the sake of an example we might consider the development in stanzas 490–512. As already indicated, this comparatively lengthy *exemplum* follows a two stanza precept (488–89) according to which the lover should ingratiate himself with people having to do with his lady and offer them money. The point of departure is the notion in stanza 489 that a monetary gift made to one of the collaborators will gain an unqualified cooperation:

> Por poquilla de cosa   del tu aver que l' dieres,
> servirte ha lealmente,   fará lo que quesieres;

---

based Endrina episode as adapted from *Ars* I, 269–70. But his comment was apparently occasioned by a faulty recension of the 12th century poem (the one included in Gustave Cohen's anthology of elegiac comedies) where vs. 72 (the corresponding passage) is given as "Quolibet et poteris ipse labore frui." In Becker's edition (a better version based on a great number of manuscripts) the same verse is given as "*Qua*libet et poteris ipse labore frui" (If you only make an effort you will enjoy any woman you want) which has far more similarity to st. 612 than *Ars* I, 269–70. One might mention as well that in the *Pamphilus* edition of Bonilla y San Martín "qualibet" is the reading given.

que poco o que mucho   dal' cada que podieres:
fará por los dineros   todo quanto pedieres.

And then begins the illustration. We might take a look at the first
two stanzas:

Mucho faz el dinero,   mucho es de amar:
al torpe faze bueno   e omne de prestar,
faze correr al coxo   e al mudo fablar,
el que non tiene manos   dineros quier tomar.

Sea un omne necio   e rudo labrador,
los dineros le fazen   fidalgo e sabidor,
quanto más algo tien   tanto es más de valor:
el que non ha dineros   non es de sí señor. (490–91)

Evident from this much alone is that the Archpriest's audience
is being offered a Spanish rendition of a "Complaint against the
Power of Money," a stock satirical theme in which the writer
laments the universal lust for money and its nefarious effect on the
social order. These pieces often contained an anticlerical dimension
and so does that of our poet. As an example we might consider
stanzas 492–93 in which don Amor laments the venality prevalent
in the church, especially the papacy:

Si tovieres dineros   avrás consolación,
plazer e alegría   e del papa ración;
comprarás paraíso,   ganarás salvación:
do son muchos dineros   es mucha bendición.

Yo vi en corte de Roma,   do es la santidat,
que todos al dinero   faziénle omildat,
grand onra le fazién,   con grand solenidat:
todos se l'encrinavan   como a la majestat.

And for an additional example we might consider stanzas 505
(506)–07 where we have an expression of regret about the general

run of clergy who are quick to grab a share in the estate of the moribund:

> Monjes, clérigos e fraires,   que aman a Dios servir,
> si barruntan que el rico   está ya para morir,
> quando oyen sus dineros   que comiençan reteñir,
> quál dellos los levará   comiençan luego a reñir:
>
> allí están esperando   quál avrá más rico tuero;
> non es muerto e ya dizen   pater noster —¡mal agüero!—
> como los cuervos al asno   quando le tiran el cuero:
> cras, cras nos lo levaremos,   ca nuestro es ya por fuero.

What is one to make of the concern demonstrated by the god of illicit sexual love for human moral failure, especially that of the clergy (all in all there are ten anticlerical stanzas in the "Complaint")? At least one critic sees in the diatribe an ironic intent.[29] But the fact remains that the theme in itself is not original. The undeniable existence of source text antecedents for don Amor's observations about money should cause one to hesitate with subjective interpretations. And the need for caution becomes all the greater if one considers that other illustrations of only partial relevance to the immediate context can be found here and there in the *Libro*. A more sound approach, therefore, would be to assume that the incongruousness of the "Complaint against the Power of Money" is simply the result of the poet's having incorporated into his *ars amandi* a preexisting piece which was not wholly suited to the surrounding context.

There is textual evidence, moreover, that the Archpriest was conscious of inconsistency and sought in one particular way to introduce an adjustment. If we look at verse *a* of stanza 513 we find the love god generalizing about the power of money:

> Las cosas que son graves fázelas de ligero.

---

[29] Cf. Anthony N. Zahareas, *The Art of Juan Ruiz, Archpriest of Hita*, pp. 99–105.

But the verse is not so much part of the "Complaint" —it ends properly with stanza 512— as rather a transitional statement allowing the poet to introduce the notions contained in the remaining verses of 513 and all of 514. What one reads is of interest: the passage goes as follows:

> Por ende a tu vieja   sey franco e llenero,
> que poco o que mucho   non vaya sin loguero:
> no m'pago de juguetes   do non anda dinero; (513bcd)

> si algo non le dieres,   cosa mucha o poca,
> sey franco de palabra,   no l'digas razón loca:
> quien non tien miel en orça,   téngala en la boca;
> mercador que esto faze   bien vende e bien troca. (514)

Stanzas 513–14 are similar in sense to 488–89 in that both sets of verse refer to an intermediary or intermediaries and mention the suitability of a monetary reward. But there is one important difference (hence the raison d'être for this modified rerun of the precept in 488–89): in 513–14 the intermediary referred to is specifically an old woman and an implication is now made that the lover need not actually confer the reward: mere talk of remuneration can be sufficient. For the poet to draw this distinction right after the "Complaint" is understandable: at an earlier point (st. 451) he had made clear that it was permissible to hold back on payment, and at a later point (815–22 in the "Endrina") he will make poignant use of the notion. It was important, therefore, to prevent the overall sense of the "Complaint,"

> el que non tien qué dar   su cavallo non corre. (512d),

from introducing an element of out and out inconsistency into the wider context of the *Libro*. One might add that this motif of welshing on payment to the go–between turns up repeatedly in *Pamphilus* related literature.[30]

---

[30] As examples we might mention the advice given to the lover in vv.

Another expansion of only partial thematic relevance to don Amor's *ars amandi* is "The Tale of the Drunken Hermit" (stanzas 530–43) which affords, as it were, a lesson in support of the precept against wine. We read of an anchorite whom the devil induced into drinking the beverage and becoming addicted. That done, the fiend persuaded him to obtain a rooster along with some hens ostensibly for telling the time of day. But when the hermit saw the rooster breeding with the hens he became sexually excited and went off to commit first a rape and then a murder (to silence his victim). He was soon apprehended and put to death.

Like so many other subordinate themes in the *Libro* "The Drunken Hermit" represents an adaptation of source material handed down from a previous age. But the plot of the Spanish version is not without a peculiar facet: as we have the story from our poet it seems to consist in a fusion of two originally different and separate narratives: on the one hand, a tale about the evils engendered by drink, and on the other, a tale of lust and repentance in which intoxication played little or no role.[31]

Just how well does the Archpriest's "twofold" exemplum suit the surrounding context? As we know, the love god advises abstention from wine because:

Buenas costumbres deves   en ti siempre aver. (528a)

The *Libro* reader is therefore bound to wonder how a story illustrative of drunkenness as conducive to assault and homicide can be apropos to the promotion of etiquette. Rather than teach a lesson about the detrimental effect of wine on a love affair, don Amor's *exemplum* seems to show how drinking can lead to uncontrollable passion and catastrophic violence. And so it should, if we consider this tale —or a certain part at any rate— for what it was originally

---

41–42 in the *Pseudo–Ars*, and the protagonist's dealings with an old woman go–between in Book II, vv. 355–96 of the *De vetula*. See also a verse epistle of Matthew of Vendôme in which an elderly go–between upbraids a seducer for his stinginess (to be found in a collection printed by W. Wattenbach in *Sitzunsberichte der bayerischen Akademie der Wissenschaften*).

[31] For the background of the tale see Lecoy, pp. 150–54.

intended to illustrate: the destructive impact of alcohol on the ascetic life: wine and a rigorous practice of self denial do not mix. In the final analysis, all "The Drunken Hermit" and the love god's precept have in common is that both concern the use of intoxicants. One might add that stanzas 530–43 constitute an instance where the secondary or contrived unity of the *Libro* comes especially to the fore.

With the conclusion of the *exemplum* our poet has not, however, exhausted everything he has to say about wine. In stanzas 544–49 we come upon some further examples of the harm done by drink. The sense is noteworthy: looking only at 544–45 we read:

> faze perder la vista   e acortar la vida;
> tira la fuerça toda   si s'toma sin medida;
> faze temblar los miembros;   todo seso olvida:
> ado es el mucho vino   toda cosa es perdida;
>
> faze oler el huelgo,   que es tacha muy mala:
> uele muy mal la boca   —non ay cosa que l'vala—,
> quema las assaduras,   el fígado trascala:
> si amar quieres dueña   el vino non te incala.

Wine, we are told, can wreck one's health and render one's presence offensive to others. Here, finally, is a statement about the effect of drinking more in accord with don Amor's "Buenas costumbres..." Indeed, in a subsequent stanza or 547 we come, once again, upon a reference to homicide as a consequence of drunkenness:

> Ado más puja el vino   qu'el seso dos meajas,
> fazen roído beudos   como puercos e grajas;
> por ende vienen muertes,   contiendas e barajas:
> el mucho vino es bueno   en cubas e en tinajas.

This time, however, the reference to killing is within a context (unruly behavior among drunkards) having more relevance to the precept than does the desperate and purposeful murder in "The Drunken Hermit."

As with the "Complaint against the Power of Money" one might try to justify this discontinuity with a subjective interpretation. But a concrete evaluation may be just as pertinent. If we take the thematic segments of the antiwine advice in sequential order we have: 1) an introductory precept or idea, followed by, 2) an illustrative expansion somewhat irrelevant to what precedes, followed by, 3) a concluding statement more properly in accord with the sense of the introductory precept (or the wider context of the *Libro*). The poet's procedure is patent: the concluding statement not only marks the end of the illustration but acts as well to offset, at least to some extent, the irrelevance. The *Libro* reader can expect, in short, to be treated here and there to a patchwork technique consisting in adjustment by way of appendage.

As indicated previously, don Amor's illustrative expansions make up a large share of the verse in his *ars amandi*. We might take stock of a numerical count: the tally is informative. Included are:

1. The portrait of an ideal female type (sts. 432–35; 444–48).[32]
2. The characteristics of a suitable go–between (sts. 436–43).
3. "The Tale of the Lazy Suitors" (sts. 457–67).
4. The "dirty joke" about Pitas Payas (sts. 474–85).
5. The "Complaint against the Power of Money" (sts. 490–510).
6. "The Tale of the Drunken Hermit" (430–543).
7. Some *facetus* type admonitions about proper comportment (554–57).

We perceive that some 77 stanzas or more than half the total in don Amor's *ars amandi* are taken up by the illustrations. And if we also give thought to the presence of thematic inconsistency we begin to wonder if one of the reasons for the existence of the love god's lesson (in essentials a skeletal outline of the *Pseudo–Ars*) was to provide a catchall for linking pieces that were previously independent. The procedure is not unique: it turns up as well in the "Garoça" (stanzas 1332–1507), one of the many brief adaptations of

---

[32] The *Pseudo–Ars* itself has such a portrait (vv. 79–104), but it differs from the one in the *Libro*.

the *Pamphilus* found throughout the *Libro*.[33] But on these "mini" presentations we shall not dwell at length. Instead, we might pass on to the "Endrina Adventure," the Spanish rendition of the *Pamphilus* as a whole and have a look at an aspect which apparently meant a good deal to our poet: he made much more of it than did the author of the source model.

---

[33] The "Garoça" is chuckfull of *exempla*. In fact, the number of stanzas they take in surpasses by far those of the plot narrative proper which is relatively short. All in all, there are nine of these reduced modified versions of the *Pamphilus* in the *Libro*, including: "una dueña" (sts. 77–104); "Cruz" (112–22); "una dueña encerrada" (167–79); "una apuesta dueña" (910–44); "una viuda loçana" (1317–20); "una dueña fermosa" (1321–1330); the "Garoça" itself (1332–1507); "una mora" (1508–12); "doña Fulana" (1619–25). Like the Garoça each was used to convey one or more incorporated or associated themes, albeit the corresponding text as we now have it is sometimes deficient. But in any case the effect of the totality is to impart to a wide range of the *Libro* the traits of an imitative Ovidian poem.

IV
The *Pamphilus*

OF THE MANY EPISODES and themes comprising the *Libro de buen amor* probably the most popular is the story of the seduction of Endrina which runs from stanza 576 to 890.[1] One can understand the preference: the reader is treated to a masterful account of illicit love followed by an implication —albeit somewhat forced— of an ethical outcome.

And yet the essentials of the plot are by no means a personal creation of our poet. As we know, stanzas 576–890 represent a vernacular rendition of the *Pamphilus*, an "elegiac comedy" often attributed to Ovid during the later Middle Ages. The reason for the attribution is patent: the play —if such we may call it— is replete with the quasi frivolous spirit of the Roman poet and contains numerous adaptations of his verse. Whoever wrote the *Pamphilus* was a skillful versifier and knew the *Ars amatoria*.

Much has been written over the years concerning the similarity of the "Endrina" to the Latin model. Some such studies are still of value, as, for example, Lecoy's collation of corresponding passages.[2] Other studies concentrate on the alterations introduced by the Archpriest and seek to explain the reason for a change. A good example is Ulrich Leo's commentary on the names given to the personæ in the Spanish version, especially that of the lover, "don

---

[1] For an outline of the plot see above p. 26-7. Traditionally st. 891 is assigned to the story proper, not the epilog. But in view of the sense it ought to be taken as part of the latter and will be treated in this chapter as such.

[2] Lecoy, pp. 307–17.

Melón de la Uerta" (the Archpriest's *nom de guerre*).[3]

Much remains, however, to be said about one particular aspect of the *Pamphilus*-Endrina dependency: the didactic purpose. We need not doubt that the Latin poem has for its goal to teach the male reader how to achieve a seduction by means of deceit and physical force. Is then the purpose of its Castilian progeny not the same? The essential similarity of protagonists and plot would seem to indicate a similarity of intent.[4]

On the other hand, beyond the narrative proper one will find a notable difference: appended to the Spanish version is an epilog running from stanza 891 through 909 in which the poet attempts to offset the flagrant amorality of the tale with a manifold palliative. But, —and here our principal matter under discussion— is it really possible to take what he says in these stanzas seriously? Or more precisely: is it really possible to render ethical a version of the *Pamphilus* (or establish an ethical purpose in retrospect) while keeping the plot essentially intact? The story would seem per se unsuited for promoting sexual restraint.

But let us defer judgement until we have considered certain relevant portions of the ""Endrina" and the full sense of the epilog. Our poet understood quite well the import of the Latin piece and knew, as is evident, which passages were especially in need of compensation. There are two of these, one dealing with the type of the go–between, and one dealing with the act of sexual contact. We shall have a look at both (in the case of the latter just the *Pam-*

---

[3] Ulrich Leo, *Zur dichterischen Originalität des Arcipreste de Hita*, pp. 51–67. A more recent study of differences is that of Dayle Seidenspinner-Núñez who sees in the Spanish rendition a deliberate magnifying of the "comic–realistic perspective" contained in the source (see pp. 38–58 in *The Allegory of Good Love: Parodic perspectivism in the* Libro de buen amor).

[4] Various critics have maintained, however, that the Archpriest had a didactic intention which was ethical. One might mention the following: Jorge Guzmán (*Una constante didáctico-moral del* Libro de buen amor); G. B. Gybbon–Monypenny, ("Dixe la por te dar ensienpro": Juan Ruiz's Adaptation of the *"Pamphilus"*); Gail Phillips (*The Imagery of the* Libro de buen amor). Broadly considered, their thesis is that the "Endrina" serves to illustrate or warn about the scheming of lovers and go–betweens.

philus version since the corresponding verses in the "Endrina" have been destroyed).

As concerns the go–between type one may say first off that the Archpriest's description, though largely his own, has a sure point of departure in the *Pamphilus* (where it forms part of the advice given by Venus). The passage goes as follows:

> Et placeat vobis interpres semper utrisque,
>   qui caute referat hoc, quod uterque cupit. (vv. 135–36)

(The two of you should always have a go–between, somebody who can do a shrewd job telling each one what he or she wants [to hear].)

A recommendation which our poet converts into Spanish this way:

> Por end busca una vieja   e buena medianera,
> que sepa sabiamente   andar esta carrera,
> que entiende de vos amos   bien la vuestra manera:
> qual don Amor te dixo,   tal sea la trotera. (st. 645)

In verses *abc* the lover is told he should look for a go–between who can deal with him and his lady as befits. This much derives from the Latin original. But the sense of the final verse stems from the Archpriest himself and constitutes a cross reference to the episode preceding the "Endrina," the "Don Amor Lecture." In that event (which also consists of an *ars amandi*) the god of love took time to elaborate on the type of an ideal intermediary. The corresponding stanzas are 436–41. For the general sense a look at 437–39 will suffice:

> Puña, en quanto puedas,   que la tu mensajera
> sea bien razonada,   sotil e costumera:
> sepa mentir fermoso   e siga la carrera,
> ca más fierbe la olla   con la su cobertera.

> Si parienta non tienes   atal, toma unas viejas
> que andan las iglesias   e saben las callejas;

> grandes cuentas al cuello,   saben muchas consejas;
> con lágrimas de Moisén   escantan las orejas;
>
> grandes maestras son   aquestas paviotas:
> andan por todo el mundo,   por plaças e por cotas,
> a Dios alçan las cuentas,   querellando sus coitas:
> ¡Ai quánto mal saben   estas viejas arlotas!

Here the reader is face to face with a summons to make use of an amoral old woman as go–between, a woman even capable of religious sham to make her way.

At first sight cynicism of this sort may appear Ovidian. The only possible parallel, however, in the amatory works of the Roman poet is the recommendation in *Ars amatoria*, I, vv. 351–98 to make use of the beloved's maid as an intermediary. But the similarity is limited. Ovid's personage is not described as an old woman, (cf. the advice not to seduce her along with the lady–love: *Ars* I, 375–98), and the verses dealing with her are comparatively few: after 398 she is never referred to again as an individual with a role of her own. In the *Pamphilus* and the *Libro*, on the other hand, the intervention of the go–between is of paramount importance: she constitutes a sine qua non of the seduction. The lover in the Latin poem tells us part of the reason why in verses 253–60, i.e., at a point right after the conversation with his lady:

> Pluribus expedior et adhuc me plura cohercent,
>   De quibus ipse meum nescio consilium.
> Si studiosus eam verbisque iocisque frequentem,
>   Auferet assuetas garrula fama vias.
> Firmet amiciciam si nulla frequencia nostram.
>   Non bene firmus adhuc forsan abibit amor.
> Usu crescit amor, omnis decrescit abusu,
>   Omnis et impastus attenuatur amor.

(Well then, I'm free from one set of predicaments. But others I don't know how to deal with continue to oppress me. If I become too eager, and chat and joke with her too often, talk and gossip will make their usual rounds. On the other hand, if I

don't keep on with the chase so that we can get closer, her love
for me, which is still not very strong, will fade. Familiarity
causes love to grow, lack of contact causes it to diminish. A
love that is not kept nourished will soon grow weak.)

The corresponding passage in the *Libro* is stanzas 688–89:

> Cuidados muchos me quexan,   a que non fallo consejo:
> si mucho uso la dueña,   con palabras de trebejo,
> pued seer tanta la fama   que salirié a concejo:
> assí perdería la dueña,   que serié pesar sobejo.
>
> si la non sigo, non uso,   el amor se perderá;
> si veye que la olvido,   ella otro amará;
> el amor con uso crece,   desusando menguará:
> do la mujer olvidares   ella te olvidará;

The lover faces a dilemma: the survival of his affaire depends on not
being seen too often in the company of his lady. By the same token
if he fails to woo her adequately, she will cease to be fond of him.
Needed, then, is a go–between. But the latter, as we presently learn,
will be more than just a messenger: she will be a woman with a
special talent for achieving her goal. In the *Pamphilus* we begin to
learn something about her when the lover states his resolve to get
in touch:

> Hic prope degit anus subtilis et ingeniosa
>   Artibus et Veneris apta ministra satis.
> Postpositis curis ad eam vestigia vertam
>   Et sibi consilium notificabo meum. (vv. 281–84)

(There's a smart quick–talking old woman who lives near here;
she knows quite well how to be of use in matters of love. So I'll
just stop worrying, go find her, and let her know what's on my
mind.)

And the Archpriest, for his part, gives two corresponding stanzas:

> Busqué trotaconventos   qual me mandó el Amor,
> de todas las maestras   escogí la mijor
> —¡Dios e la mi ventura,   que me fue guiador!—,
> acerté en la tienda   del sabio corredor.
>
> Fallé una tal vieja   qual avía mester,
> artera e maestra   e de mucho saber;
> doña Venus por Pánfilo   non pudo más fazer
> de quanto fizo ésta   por me fazer plazer. (697–98)

To which he adds two other stanzas which are independent of the model and elaborate on the character of the go–between:

> Era vieja bohona   de las que venden joyas:
> éstas echan el lazo,   éstas cavan las foyas;
> non ay tales maestras   como estas viejas croyas:
> éstas dan la maçada;   si as orejas, oyas;
>
> como lo an de uso   estas tales bohonas,
> andan de casa en casa   vendiendo muchas donas:
> non se reguardan dellas,   están con las personas,
> fazen con mucho viento   andar las atahonas. (699–700)

An unscrupulous old trickster along the lines recommended by don Amor. Noteworthy in particular is her aptitude for mendacity and deception (437c, 699bc). What could be more in conflict with the traditional Christian approach to sexuality (aside, of course, from the use of physical force which in any case will soon take place)? But our poet was careful to protect himself: in verse d of stanza 699 he tells his audience: "si as orejas, oyas;", an expression similar in part to one used in the palliative at the end of the story. Of this passage we shall presently have more to say. For the moment suffice it to observe that the type of the go–between was apparently considered so nefarious as to require an immediate allusion (albeit a slight one) to a moralizing intention.

If we turn our attention now to the act of sexual intimacy we find that the episode exists in the *Pamphilus*, but not in any of the *Libro* manuscripts. Or more precisely, at the corresponding locus the reader will encounter a lacuna, which in *S*, the most complete of the codices, occurs between stanzas 877 and 878.[5] Various scholars have attributed the gap to haphazard damage, as, for example, the loss (whatever the cause) of a page at one point leading to the loss of an additional page at another point.[6] This view is not without a certain pertinence: several lacunas found in the *Libro* may have come about accidentally. But even so, there is good reason to believe that a willful suppression of verse between 877 and 878 took place.

To begin with, one need not doubt that the verse in question conveyed an incident of sexual contact. That such is the case can be readily determined from the content of 877 and 878. In the former we find the lover speaking to his lady in the house of the intermediary (he has just come in and pretends to be surprised at her presence there):

> ¡Señora doña Endrina!,   ¡vos, la mi enamorada!;
> vieja, ¡por esto teníades   a mí la puerta cerrada!
> ¡tan buen día es oy éste   que fallé atal celada!
> Dios e mi buena ventura   me la tovieron guardada.

The *Pamphilus* equivalent consists of a medley of the sense conveyed by verses 661 and 667–68:

> "O Galathea, mea super omnia causa salutis,
>
> Huc mea direxit felix vestigia casus,
>   Nam tenet iste locus hoc, quod amo melius!"

(Galathea, you alone can bring me back to health;

What real good luck it was that caused me to come here, a place

---

[5] Three principal manuscripts underlie modern editions of the Libro: *S* (Salamanca), *T* (Toledo), and *G* (Gayoso). All three lack the stanzas in question.

[6] M. R. Lida, for instance, suggests in one of her studies (*Dos obras maestras españolas*, p. 53) that the loss of verse may not be the result of expurgation.

where I find the one I love most.)

And looking now at 878 or the first stanza on the other side of the gap we find the go–between replying to a complaint made by Endrina about something presumably sexual and untoward:

> Quando yo salí de casa,   pues que veyedes las redes
> ¿por qué fincávades sola,   con él, entre estas paredes?
> A mí non rebtedes fija,   que vos vos lo merecedes:
> el mijor cobro que tiene   vuestro mal, que lo calledes;

An equivalent for the preceding stanza does not exist in the *Pamphilus*. But the absence is no indication that the plot of the "Endrina" differed notably. The verses are part of the Archpriest's personal expansion of the go–between's reply (vv. 741–50 in the model version). A direct dependency resumes with stanza 883: the words are Endrina's who speaks once again and continues to utter her complaint.[7]:

> Si las aves lo podiessen   bien saber e entender
> quántos de lazos les paran,   non las podrían prender;
> ya quando el lazo veyen   ya las lievan a vender:
> mueren por el poco cevo,   non se pueden defender;

Surely one of the more poignant stanzas in the *Libro*. The equivalent in the model text goes this way:

> Sic piscis curuum iam captus percipit hamum,
>   Sic avis humanos capta videt laqueos. (vv. 763–64)

(And so it is that the fish, once caught, notices the bent hook; and the bird, once caught, perceives the traps set by men.)

---

[7] In the Latin model the order of speeches after the sexual incident are as follows: Pamphilus, then the go–between, then Galathea, then the go–between (within which the Libro version starts again), then Pamphilus, then Galathea, then the go–between.

It would appear, then, that some form of sexual impropriety had taken place in the missing stanzas.

But why the overlap? If a scabrous episode was suppressed between stanzas 877 and 878, for what reason were other stanzas of a less offensive nature, i.e., those comprising Endrina's initial complaint to the go–between and part of the go–between's reply eliminated as well?[8] To all lights the cause had to do with insensitivity: the expurgator proceeded in ruthless fashion: rather than restrict himself to the offending verses he removed entire leaves. The evidence is hard to dispute: stanza 877 is located at the bottom of folio 51 verso while 878 is located at the top of folio 52 recto and the antique numbering of folios jumps from LVIII to LXI. Two leaves, then, containing a total of 32 stanzas (eight per side, as is usual in the *S* manuscript) were suppressed. Lost is the erotic incident plus a certain number of additional verses which happened to occur within the limits of folios LVIX and LX.[9]

At this point it would be well to have a look at the offending verses as they are in the *Pamphilus* (vv. 681–96: the lady–love is speaking and voicing her objection to Pamphilus' physical advances):

> "Pamphile, tolle manus! Te frustra nempe fatigas,
>   Nil valet iste labor, quod petis, esse nequit.
> Pamphile, tolle manus! Male nunc offendis amicam.
>   Iamque redibit anus: Pamphile, tolle manus!
> Heu michi, quam parvas habet omnis femina vires,
>   Quam leviter nostras vincis utrasque manus!

---

[8] Also occurring within this range are two speeches of Pamphilus. But the first one (its locus is right after the episode of sexual contact) may have been considered offensive and hence intended for expurgation. The second one our poet may have excluded from the Spanish version for his own reason.

[9] The preceding factors in combination with the sense of vv. 681–96 in the *Pamphilus* —the passage would have been by far the most sexually provocative in the *Libro*— make it difficult to believe that the loss of stanzas between 877 and 878 was accidental. For some concise commentary covering all the points see the *Libro* edition of G. B. Gybbon–Monypenny, p. 289.

Pamphile, nostra tuo cur pectore pectora ledis?
  Quod sic me tractas, est scelus atque nephas.
Desine! Clamabo! Quid agis? Male detegor a te.
  Perfida, me miseram, quando redibit anus?
Surge, precor: nostras audit vicinia lites.
  Que tibi me credit, non bene fecit anus.
Ulterius tecum me non locus iste tenebit
  Nec me decipiet, ut modo fecit, anus.
Huius victor eris facti, licet ipsa relucter,
  Sed tamen inter nos rumpitur omnis amor." (681–96)

(Pamphilus, get your hands off me! You're wasting your
time. This is no good; what you want is impossible. Pamphilus,
get your hands off me! You're offending me terribly. The old
woman will soon be back. Pamphilus, get your hands off me!
How awful, women have so little strength: how easy it is for
you to keep my hands from resisting. Pamphilus why are you
hurting me? You are pressing too heavily against my breast. It's
awful, it's terrible to treat me like this. Stop! I'm going to
scream. What are you doing? How dare you undress me! Oh, I've
been done in. When is that treacherous old woman going to
come back? Please get up; the neighbors can hear what's going
on. She did a rotten thing handing me over to you. You'll never
catch me again in this place with you. That old woman will
never trick me again as she did this time. Alright, you'll be the
winner and have your way, although I did put up a good fight.
But our love, of course, is over and finished.)

Do we have here an example of acquaintance rape? Or is it an
instance of "The lady says no, but really means yes"? The pathos of
the passage would seem to indicate the former. The beloved,
moreover, never alters her resolve to break with the protagonist: she
remains outraged to the end. But whatever the case, the Archpriest
himself clearly thought his Spanish equivalent was at risk. In his
epilog he took care to include statements intended either to palliate
what went before or disown responsibility outright. To these
assertions we shall now give some thought.

All in all, the reader will encounter in the corresponding stanzas

(891–909) four lines of defense. They are as follows:

1. The affaire of the lovers ended in marriage (891ab).
2. The offensive aspect of the story was (originally) written by someone else, not by our poet himself (891cd).
3. The story was written to warn the ladies of the peril involved in trusting a lover and his go–between (892–908, 909acd and the first hemistich of b).
4. The lover–protagonist was someone else, not our poet himself (the second hemistich of 909b).

At first sight heavy artillery indeed! Upon careful consideration, however, one notices a good deal that is specious. Not only are the four defensive devices weak in themselves, but become even more so when considered for their relationship to each other.

Thus, reflecting on 891ab we perceive that the device is unsuited to the general sense of the "Endrina" (and the *Pamphilus* as well). The two lines go as follows:

> Doña Endrina e don Melón   en uno casados son:
> alégranse las campañas   en las bodas, con razón.

The couple, we are told, got married. But how is one to relate this assertion to the story itself where the lover nowhere says he intends to marry his lady?[10] On the contrary, at the only point where he alludes to ultimate domestic arrangements he has this to say:

> Fasta que su marido   pueble el cementerio
> non casará conmigo,   que serié adulterio; (795ab)

The reader may suppose at first that "casará conmigo" signifies a marriage. But from the context it is clear that the expression refers to concubinage (a possible implication of *casar*). Likewise, the *ars*

---

[10] For her part the go–between, when speaking to Endrina, mentions marriage on several occasions. But anything the old woman has to say should, of course, be understood as a ruse.

amandi of doña Venus (and that of the love goddess in the Latin original) is strictly a program for seduction, not marriage. As the goddess summarizes just before taking leave of the anxious lover:

> Amigo, en este fecho,   que quieres más que t' diga:
> sey sotil e acucioso   e avrás tu amiga; (648ab)

Nothing here of matrimony. And yet in the final stanza of the story (890) the go–between tells the lovers they should marry:

> Pues que por mí dezides   que el daño es venido,
> por mí quiero que sea   el vuestro bien avido:
> vos seet mujer suya   e él vuestro marido;
> todo vuestro deseo   es bien por mí cumplido.

A recommendation based on verse 778 in the *Pamphilus* (shortly before the end):

> Hec tua sit coniunx, vir sit et iste tuus!

(She [addressing Pamphilus] should be your wife, he [adressing Galathea] should be your husband.)

But is this a recommendation to be taken seriously? One should bear in mind that in the *Pamphilus* —where a true marriage finale would be as malapropos as in the "Endrina"— nothing is said to the effect that the lovers married; the notion is limited to a suggestion put forth by the go–between. What the author does is present his reader with calculated indecisiveness: to defend the story he introduces an allusion to a marriage ending, i.e., an allusion to an ethical ending, but without going so far as to state that a marriage actually took place. He manages, as it were, to "have his cake and eat it too."

In the *Libro* version we have an out and out affirmation of matrimony: not only is there a suggestion by the go–between in the final stanza that the lovers should marry, but in the following stanza (the first in the epilog–palliative) the suggestion becomes a fait accompli. It would seem that our poet thought his rendition of the *Pamphilus* was in need of a more categorical defense. Time would prove him right: the suppression of verse between 878 and 879 affords evidence. But sexual propriety is one thing, narrative plausibility another. From the standpoint of credibility the marriage denouement remains artificial, an appendage motivated by an extraneous design.[11]

Looking now at the poet's device conveyed by 891cd we read:

Si villanía he dicho   aya y de vos perdón,
que lo feo de la estoria   dize Pánfilo e Nasón. (891cd)

A statement which can "cover" the scene of sexual contact: somebody else, we are told, was (originally) responsible for the offensive aspect of the story, i.e., our poet did not create it, what he did was pass it on. Nothing here, of course, which might in itself diminish responsibility. But if the story as a whole served some ethically constructive purpose, and transmitting "lo feo" were a necessary concomitant, then, doubtless, a certain viability could be attributed to the disclaimer.

Can it be said, however, that the "Endrina" serves this kind of purpose? If we look at the next in order of the four devices we find the poet telling us that it does. The corresponding stanzas run from 892 through 909 (though not including the second hemistich of 909b). For the gist we need only consider 892ab and 904–05:

Dueñas, abrit orejas,   oít lición,
entendet bien las fablas: guardadvos del varón;

Assí, señoras dueñas,   entendet el romance
guardadvos de amor loco   non vos prenda ni alcance:
abrit vuestras orejas,   el coraçon se lance
en amor de Dios limpio,   loco amor non le trance;

---

[11] Corominas (p. 344) sees the expression "en uno casados son" in v. 891a as referring to concubinage. But the point is not well taken. Would the modest ladylove, who constantly expresses concern for her reputation, consent to a public celebration of a shack up? In all probability the verb *casar* as used in 891a (unlike the use in 795b) indicates a marriage.

> la que por aventura   es o fue engañada
> guárdese que non torne   al mal otra vegada:
> de coraçón e orejas   non quiera ser menguada,
> en ajena cabeca   sea bien castigada;

Women are to learn a lesson from the "Endrina": they should beware of men and beware of "amor loco"; they should dedicate themselves to a pure love, to a love of God; especially the woman who is or was deceived (by a man) should take care not to relapse. According to our poet, therefore, the Spanish version serves to warn the ladies about the depredations of men and "amor loco." Is that, however, a message made clear in the "Endrina" itself? Nowhere in the course of the narrative do we read that the piece is intended as an exposé of male philandering. At most, there is "si as orejas, oyas;" in the second hemistich of 699d, an expression similar to one used several times in the palliative.[12] But in 699d there is no reference to women and the similarity comes to mind much later in retrospect. A comment made by Leo on the character of the poet's epilog goes to the heart of the matter: "He did well to give us his assurance (that sound instruction was present in the story); the unprepared reader would have looked to no avail in the Endrina episode for a useful lesson, especially one for young women."[13]

The supposed instruction meant for the ladies is, of course, simply the obverse of the instruction intended for the men, i.e., women should take stock of the stratagems practiced by the lover and avoid being deceived and dishonored. One might, perhaps, incline to consider this appended reversal as too facile, a didactic "cheap shot." The assessment would have a certain validity: as already indicated, nothing in the way of a clear and sure antici-

---

[12] The expression has an idiomatic ring and occurs elsewhere in differing forms (162d; 604c). One might add here that much of the epilog consists in an *exemplum*, the "Ensiemplo del asno sin coraçon e sin orejas" (892–903). Likewise part of the "Endrina" proper is given over to several exempla: the "De la abutarda y de la golondrina" (746–53c) and the "Assentóse el lobo" (766–79: the text is defective). We have seen this kind of creative intermixture before in the "Don Amor Lecture."

[13] Leo, p. 47.

pation turns up within the narrative.[14]

But abrupt or not, the Archpriest's advice to the ladies contains another and more problematic fault: inconsistency among the defensive devices themselves. Given that the lovers marry in the "Endrina," can one still say the heroine has been done a disservice? We have seen that the author of the Latin poem was able to create an equivocal outcome by combining sexual aggression with an indecisive reference to marriage. Our poet, however, goes the full distance, as it were, and represents the lover as having sexual designs on the heroine, but in the end as definitely united to her in matrimony. What, then, is the lesson to be learned? If we are to take the poet at his word ("Doña Endrina e don Melón en uno casados son"), may we not conclude that the "Endrina" demonstrates a method for getting married?

Or, if all of this seems perplexing, would the reader do better to not take the palliative seriously? The last of the four defensive devices has a bearing on the question. It consists of the second hemistich of 909b (which turns up within the stanzas comprising the third device):

díxela por dar ensiemplo,   mas non porque a mí avino;

The events narrated previously, we are told, did not happen to the Archpriest personally. One need not, of course, have supposed they did in the sense of a true occurrence: the story is an invention, a Spanish rendition of a source text. But that is for the audience to know on its own: our poet consistently relates the events as if they

---

[14] From the standpoint of traditional Christian morality (to which, presumably, the Archpriest subscribed) the "Endrina" must be set down as inherently unsuitable as a lesson in promotion of feminine chastity or an expose of sexual wantonness. The fact remains that the story is erotic and provides instruction in successful philandering. This lesson (especially with its former explicit component) easily overwhelms any others whether real or pretended. Our poet had no illusions. Hence his protracted and insistent epilog. But the eventual censor had no illusions either. One might recall Marbod's observation concerning the effect of provocative reading on a pupil (p. 22, above).

had come from his own experience. Or is it, perhaps, that he does not want the audience to confound the fictional protagonist in the "Endrina" with himself as fictional protagonist in the rest of the *Libro*? For clarification one need only consider stanza 608 of the "Endrina" in conjunction with stanza 423 of the preceding episode, "The Don Amor Lecture." In 608 Venus says this to the lover at the start of her *ars amandi*:

> ya fueste consejado   del Amor, mi marido,
> dél en muchas maneras   fueste apercebido,
> porque l' fueste sañudo   contigo poco estido;
> de mí será lo qu' él   no t' dixo repetido.

The stanza refers back to the debate between the protagonist and don Amor in 181 through 575. As we know, the first half (roughly) of the exchange consists in a series of angry accusations directed at the god of love, and the second half in a reply ("The Don Amor Lecture") which begins with stanza 423. These latter four verses go as follows:

> El Amor, con mesura,   diome respuesta luego:
> "Arcipreste, sañudo   non seas, yo te ruego,
> non digas mal de amor   en verdat nin en juego:
> que a las veces poca agua   faze abaxar grand fuego.

There can be no doubt: our poet has sought to identify the lover-protagonist of the "Endrina Episode" with the "Arcipreste" of the "Don Amor Lecture," i.e., with none other than himself as portrayed in the rest of the *Libro*.[15] Why then the denial in 909b? There are three possibilities:

---

[15] See also 576a, 609ab, 645d, 697a and 845a vis a vis 19bc. M. R. Lida maintains (*Estudios de literatura española y comparada*, pp. 17–19) that the lover in the "Endrina" is not the Archpriest. And yet the large number of verses indicative of the contrary renders her position untenable. Her interpretation, for that matter, does nothing less than rip the guts out of the plot in this part of the *Libro*.

1) The poet is asserting that the protagonist's pursuit of Endrina is not a historical reality. And most certainly it is not. And yet he has spoken to his audience from 576 (or better, from 181) onwards as if he were recounting personal past events. The result is that the sense of the second hemistich of 909b is either abrupt and superfluous, or, if not, then at variance with the narrative as it is given down to the start of the epilog.

2) The poet is asserting that the protagonist of the "Don Amor Lecture" and the protagonist of the "Endrina" are different personæ, a contention which flies in the face of 608 vis-á-vis 423 and numerous other declarations as well.

3) The poet's assertion has no true logical or consequential relationship to what went before. Its function is that of an independent disclaimer for the sexual impropriety which had been related.

The third alternative would be the most feasible. The Archpriest is telling his audience to disregard all that went before with reference to "arcipreste" (or some other identifying expression) and consider him extraneous to the events in the "Endrina." From the standpoint of continuity the verse lacks for sense. But to maintain a tight cohesion was apparently not the intention of our poet. What mattered was putting distance *après coup* between himself and his autobiographic rendition of the *Pamphilus*. True consequence counted for less.

The procedure is hardly unique. We have already seen an example of an unlikely denouement serving as moral compensation for a risqué dialog (the "Te mihi meque tibi"). For another example of an epilog of dubious relevance to the primary composition we might consider the *Pamphilus* influenced *Rota Veneris* of Boncompagno da Signa.[16] In this 13th century combination of *ars amandi* and model letters (a mock demonstration of the *ars dictaminis*) one can find an epistolary exchange between a nun and a male admirer.[17] A summary of the letters (three in all) would be

---

[16] A partial edition of the text along with commentary was published by Carl Sutter in 1894. An English version of the entirety prepared by Joseph Purkart appeared in 1975.

[17] On pp. 90–92 in Sutter.

useful since they are illustrative of the overall spirit of the work.

In the first letter the nun writes in response to the amatory attention of the admirer. She tells him she is surprised he would seek to associate with her as she has vowed her virginity to the Heavenly Spouse. She wears the black veil and therefore has a special form of mortality. He does wrong to find her attractive. But the devil has such power over him that he does not hesitate to violate a bride of the Lord. He will not succeed.

In the second letter the admirer replies that he desires to share in her special form of mortality. If her veil is black, her body underneath is probably white. Her Spouse is heavenly, but that is a matter concerning the soul, not the body. As for her accusation that he does not hesitate to violate a bride of the Lord, he must reply that she is right. After all, the Lord has caused the death of his relatives and causes rain and hail to fall on him.

In the third letter the nun concedes he has persuaded her. The two should feign an outward enmity but secretly enjoy the delights of love. As for the violation of a heavenly bride, she will gladly grant him what he wants. That way he can always get revenge for the wrongs done to him by the Lord.

Here as elsewhere, an extraordinary degree of scurrilousness. But if Boncompagno knew how to get a laugh he also knew how to defend his *Rota Veneris*. At the end of the composition is an epilog which goes as follows:[18]

Licet autem plura, que lasciviam ostendere videantur, in hoc opere proposuerim, non tamen est credibile me fuisse aut velle fore lascivum. Nam Salomon, qui meruit assistrici dei id est eius sapientie copulari, multa proposuit in Canticis canticorum que si secundum litteram intelligerentur, magis possent ad carnis voluptatem quam ad moralitatem trahi. Verum tamen sapientes dubia in meliorem partem interpretantur, dicentes sponsam vel amicam ecclesiam fuisse, sponsum Jhesum Christum. Credere igitur debetis, quod Boncompagnus non dixit

---

[18] Quoted as in Sutter, p. 96.

hoc alicuius lascivie causa, set sociorum precibus amicabiliter condescendit.

(Although I have set forth in this work much that seems to demonstrate lewdness, nonetheless, [you should] not think that I was or wish to be lascivious. Salomon who was worthy, as you know, to be joined to the adjuvant of God, that is, to His wisdom, set forth many things in his Song of Songs which, if understood in a literal sense, would more readily lead to the delights of the flesh than to morality. And yet those who are wise interpret questionable things in a higher sense and say that the spouse or the lady friend was the church and the husband was Christ. And so you should believe that Boncompagno did not say [all] this for the sake of some lewdness, but that he yielded in kindness to the pleas of his friends.)

An allegorical approach, as the author implies, would be in order. Also, it was not his intention to treat of sexual matters: his friends obliged him to do so. But who can take seriously statements like these under the circumstance? The *Rota Veneris* is jam packed with farcical humor and parody, a characteristic which seems to exclude the possibility of an allegorical interpretation in the usual Christian sense (exposition of transcendental beliefs thought to be ascertainable upon reflection). Indeed —an ineluctable result— the epilog, by force of association, becomes itself suspect of humor or parody. One need say no more.

But still, be it ever so superficial, the epilog constitutes a conspicuous moralizing affirmation. The upshot is that the reader —we have seen this effect before— "can have his cake and eat it too": on the one hand he can amuse himself with a libertine composition, but on the other hand feel assured in the end that his reading matter had an upright component.

The same may be said for the Archpriest's version of the *Pamphilus*. The audience, having heard or read the "Endrina," may rest assured in the long run that the lovers got married, that the poet was not the inventor of a scandalous episode, nor himself the lover–protagonist, and that the story serves to warn women about the evil caused by suitors and go–betweens.

Did credibility count then for nothing? Clearly any question concerning the acceptability of a fictional narrative and related comments will touch upon the type of public for which it was intended. Who were the contemporary readers or listeners of the "Endrina" and the Latin source model? We need not bother here with a lengthy discussion of the social condition of the Archpriest's audience. Suffice it to say there is much in the *Libro* suggestive of minstrelsy (*juglaría*) and hence of orientation toward a jongleur recital at popular gatherings.[19] Such recitals were not always bound to a specific version of a given piece: it was possible to make additions or alterations as thought fit. Our poet himself gave approval to the procedure if done by someone competent. In stanza 1629 he tells us:

> Qualquier omne que l' oya,   si bien trobar sopiere,
> puede i más añedir   e emendar si quisiere:
> ande de mano en mano   a quienquier que l' pediere
> como pella a las dueñas: tómelo quien podiere.

In the *Libro* we have a text admittedly amorphous. Changes are permissible, changes which may vary according to the circumstance. Any problem, therefore, with credibility (and other difficulties) is readily resolved: a given audience may be presented with that which is deemed most suitable. Or simply that which is deemed most likely to please.

In contrast the *Pamphilus* is conveyed by a hard and fast manuscript tradition (aside, of course, from the customary scribal variants) and the readership can easily be established: as a result of the language employed circulation was restricted to members of the clergy (give or take a bit).[20]   Also, the go–between's marriage

---

[19] For minstrels and minstrelsy in general one might consult the magisterial *Poesía juglaresca* of R. Menéndez Pidal. See especially Chapter VIII (6th ed.) for minstrel performances with a bearing on the *Libro*.

[20] The same language which acted to protect this "elegiac comedy" from censorship (might one not speak of the piece as "inside" literature?). On the other hand, the "Endrina," composed as it was in the vernacular and intended for a wider audience, had to face hostility.

recommendation presents no great problem with credibility: it may be taken with a grain of salt: the poet does not say that the lovers actually married.

It was essential moreover to avoid having the love affaire in this elegiac comedy end in matrimony. The author knew his business: an unequivocal marriage finale would not only lack for believability, but would constitute something of a disappointment for the typical reader. It could hardly be otherwise. In reality the story of Pamphilus and Galathea corresponds to the sexual predicament of the clerical rank and file. On the one hand, ecclesiastics were unable to contract a legal marriage. On the other hand, those who took to promiscuity usually had little to fear from church authorities: what mattered was not that the clergy be chaste, but that they be unmarried.[21] Discretion, therefore, was the order of the day for the philandering cleric: much might be condoned provided there was no outcry.

In this light we can better understand the great appeal of the *Pamphilus* during the late Middle Ages. The story is one of hidden love, a love that begins with a secretive wooing, continues with a resort to a go–between, and concludes with a clandestine sexual encounter. The success at seduction, however, is primarily dependent on the intervention of the go–between: she represents an ideal type of collaborator for the lover who seeks a liaison, but must keep his affaire out of the public eye. One is tempted to believe that many a clergyman who spent time reading the poem was able to identify personally —if only in spirit— with the situations and events set forth. We know for certain that our Archpriest did: he used his Spanish version to portray himself as a veritable Iberian Pamphilus. He also took care to contrive and append some justification.

---

[21] For enforced celibacy see the old but standard *History of Sacerdotal Celibacy in the Christian Church* of H. C. Lea, esp. vol. I, pp. 434–50. Unmarried clergy were, of course, cheaper to maintain and less likely to side with political ambitions at variance with those of the papacy

V
De Vetula

TO WHAT GENRE CAN we assign the *Libro* as a whole? Is there a preexisting type? Or is the poem perhaps sui generis? On the one hand we have episodes and themes which sometimes lack for mutual compatibility; in places one even notices the presence of contextual confusion. On the other hand we have an autobiographic pretense which runs the length of the work and provides —with varying degrees of success— a connecting link over most of the ensemble. General unity, in short, would seem both present and absent at the same time. The critical reader is therefore likely to wonder: was the formation of the *Libro* unique, or was there a precedent?

The first commentator to make a serious attempt to fix the *Libro* within a previously existing tradition was Américo Castro.[1] According to this former dean of Hispanists an adequate interpretation of the Archpriest's poem must proceed from the premise that the work is a compound of Western and Arabic elements, the creation of an artist who was familiar with both sides of the cultural divide. And doubtless, to some extent the proposition is sound: for evidence of the presence of Islam in the *Libro* one need only consider the poet's use of Arabic expressions in stanzas 1508–12, and his assessment of musical instruments in 1516–17.

The proposals made by Castro concerning the role of Islamic philosophy and literature in the *Libro* are many and manifold. Of interest for us here, however, are his two contentions that 1) the

---

[1] Castro's comments can be found in his *España en su historia. Cristianos, moros y judíos*, pp. 371–469.

autobiography in the *Libro* is of Arabic origin, and 2) Ibn Hazm's treatise on sexual love, *The Dove's Neck Ring* (11th century), was used as a model for the Spanish poem.[2]

How strong are these views? Underlying the first contention is the notion that medieval Arabic literature contains a good deal of erotic autobiography while medieval Western literature does not. But the consensus among experts is otherwise: on the whole, Moslems were just as disinclined as Christians to draw up a history of their personal sexual life.[3] A certain few willing to do so did exist, but they are the exception, not the rule. Castro's position is built on exaggeration.

What can one say of the *Libro–Dove's Neck Ring* dependency? To demonstrate the relationship is particularly imperative for Castro since in his view the Arabic composition constitutes (like the *Libro*) an example of erotic autobiography. And yet, in this respect too, we encounter exaggeration: rather than an autobiography, *The Dove's Neck Ring* is essentially a treatise on sexual love enriched on occasion with anecdotes from the author's experience. The deficiency is not so great, however, as to nullify Castro's proposal: the anecdotes may still have served as a catalyst for the amatory episodes in the *Libro* (assuming for the moment that the Archpriest knew the Muslim work).

More importantly, Castro adduces in support of the dependency various passages in the Spanish poem which constitute, as he maintains, a borrowing from the Arabic treatise (they can be found here and there throughout his study, but especially on pp. 404–15). For the sake of an example we might consider the following comparison dealing with the effects of love:[4]

---

[2] See Castro, pp. 402 and 404ff. An English translation of *The Dove's Neck Ring* was published by A. R. Nykl in 1931.

[3] Cf. G. B. Gybbon–Monypenny, "Autobiography in the *Libro de buen amor* in the Light of Some Literary Comparisons," pp. 64–65.

[4] The passages are cited as in Castro (pp. 408–09). The page numbers which accompany the quotations from *The Dove's Neck Ring* refer to Nykl's translation (the quotations were apparently done into Spanish by Castro himself).

LIBRO
"El amor faz sotil al ome que es rudo (156a)

...

al ome que es covarde, fázelo muy atrevudo (156c)

...

e al viejo faz perder mucho la vejez. (157b)

...

El que es enamorado, por muy feo que sea,
otrosí su amiga, maguer que sea muy fea,
el uno e el otro non ha cosa que vea,
que tan bien le paresca nin que tanto desea; (158)

El bavieca ...
a su amiga bueno paresçe ... (159ab)

toda cosa que dize paresçe mucho buena; (164b)

DOVE'S NECK RING
"Un zote se hace inteligente ... un cobarde se hace bravo ...
un viejo recobra la mocedad llena de brío," etc. (p. 16).
El amor ciega el juicio del enamorado:
"El amante se maravilla de lo que dice el amado, aun cuando
ello sea el colmo del absurdo y de lo inaudito ... lo cree hasta
cuando miente" (p. 15).

Castro describes the verses he has drawn from *Libro* stanzas 156
and 157 as having a literal relationship to the corresponding passage
in *The Dove's Neck Ring*. And they do indeed show a strong
similarity. But problems exist: the literalness is gained by an
eclectic reduction and rearrangement of correspondences. Also
—this above all— the notion conveyed is part and parcel of a
Courtly Love commonplace, "the ennobling effect of love." We have
seen the idea before in the *De amore* of Andreas Capellanus where
one finds a rendition just as similar in expression and sense to the
Libro equivalent. And so it goes: one correspondence after another
reveals a relationship open to question: if the similarity of wording
is not contrived, then either the concept is known to other Chris-

tian writers or reference is made to a phenomenon common to both sides of the religious frontier. On balance there would seem to be no direct connection between the passages cited.[5]

But still, is it possible that the Archpriest had at least a vague indirect knowledge of *The Dove's Neck Ring*?[6] Even this appears uncertain. The treatise was largely unknown to Spanish Arabs both in the time of the author and later in the 14th–century. One can understand why: the book is aristocratic and exquisite, a work of art composed for a select few (only one manuscript has come down to us). If such then was the case in the Muslim zone in the 1300s, who in the Christian zone during the same century would have been familiar with the composition? Formal testimony to the effect that anyone did is lacking.

Castro was not the only scholar of distinction to associate the structure of the *Libro* with non–Christian literature. In a number of publications M. R. Lida sought to place the Spanish masterpiece in the tradition of the Hebrew makama.[7] More exactly, this Argentine commentator pointed to a particular manifestation of the type, *The Book of Delight*, written in the 12th century by a Barcelona rabbi, Yosef Ben Meir ibn Zabara.

According to what we read in Lida's studies, Ben Meir's work and the *Libro* have the following (chief) aspects in common:[8]

---

[5] For the opinion of an Arabist see pp. 77–82 in the introduction to a translation of the treatise prepared by E. García Gómez. The correspondences are deemed inconclusive.

[6] Castro concedes (p. 402) that our poet's knowledge may have been gained via oral transmission.

[7] For her comments on the *Libro* see *Dos obras maestras españolas*, pp. 11–62, and *Estudios de literatura española y comparada*, pp. 14–91.

[8] Cf. *Estud. de lit.*, pp 23–27. Lida's books are tersely written and packed with erudition. But since the *Libro* differs notably in many respects from *The Book of Delight* and our poet never mentions the Hebrew work nor the makama, much of Lida's commentary has little value as evidence for establishing a dependency. The most one can do on behalf of this Judaizing view is to show a close similarity in structure or theme and indicate a possible manner of derivation. Only the basics, so to speak, are viable. All the rest floats or sinks in tow. One might add here that an English translation of *The Book of Delight* (with an informative introduction) was

1. The presence of an autobiographic pretense which binds together a large number of subordinate themes and motifs.
2. The presence in both works of various subordinate themes and motifs which are similar.

At first sight Lida seems to make a fair case for a dependency of the *Libro* on *The Book of Delight*. Upon close evaluation, however, one notices problems. To start off, there is a hitch with the events narrated in the autobiography: *The Book of Delight* contains not a single amatory or erotic episode. The deficiency is serious since sexual pursuit is of the essence in the *Libro* narration. But Lida is able to compensate: she indicates that other works of makama contained such stories and mentions the *Tahkemoni* of Jehudah Al Harizi and the *Neum Asher ben Yehudah* of Solomon Tzakbel.[9] At which point the careful reader will pause to reflect: in reality the proposed model for the *Libro* consists of a number of compositions. Are these comodels also autobiographic in the sense of a personal history of the author (whether real or pretended)? Lida has little to say in this respect, but the fact is *they are not.* Her proposal obliges one to believe therefore that the principal facet of autobiography in the *Libro* was based on works which were other than autobiographic.

As for the subordinate themes and motifs common to both the *Libro* and *The Book of Delight*, Lida adduces a great number on page 23 and the top of 24 in her *Estudios de literatura.* They include: explanatory and dedicatory pieces (in lyrical verse at the beginning of the work, in rhymed prose at the end), a giant who plays the role of interlocutor with the protagonist, a debate in pro and contra concerning a trip, the protagonist's willingness to undertake a trip, the many faceted trip itself, and a subsequent sense of homesickness. Farther down on page 24 we have these: a taste for scriptural

---

published by Moses Hadas in 1932.

[9] *Estud. de lit.*, p. 24. At this point Lida mentions the authors only, not the title of their respective works which she generalizes as "otras maqamat." But let there be no mistake: these are separate and independent compositions. For a brief analysis of both see Israel Zinberg, *A History of Jewish Literature*, pp. 166–68 and 170–73.

reminiscences, aphorisms, instructional disquisitions, tales, fables, anecdotes, liturgical parodies, a dissertation on the art of physiognomy, a description of a woman tantamount to caricature, a humorous portrait based on antithesis and verbal paradox, an attack on wine drinking, a litany of name calling directed at a companion, jokes, a pervading bourgeois spirit, and restraint in demonstrating rhetorical and grammatical virtuosity.

Certainly a formidable array of correspondences. And yet many are too unspecific to carry weight. The use of tales, fables, and anecdotes, for example, was common in medieval Christian literature. And what is more, a close look at any and all of the correspondences reveals differences that tend to diminish the similarity. For a case in point one might give thought again to the fables: without exception those in *The Book of Delight* differ from those in the *Libro*.[10] For another case in point one might consider Lida's comparison of the personage said to be a giant in *The Book of Delight* with don Amor in the *Libro* (represented by the Archpriest as tall): too much is made of too little: don Amor is not a giant, he is simply tall and handsome:

un omne gran, fermoso,   mesurado, a mí vino; (181c)

Not so with Enan (the giant in *The Book of Delight*) who is portrayed as a fire breathing demon.[11] If he is a giant, that is a facet of his horrendous demonic condition. The correspondence hardly exists.

Another important weakness in Lida's proposal is the absence in the *Libro* of a reference to *The Book of Delight* or the *Tahke-moni* or the *Neum Asher ben Yehudah*. Our poet, to be sure, has certain Western sources which go unnamed. But one can readily demonstrate their presence in the *Libro*. As an example we might mention the fables once again; the majority stem beyond doubt from

---

[10] For a list of the fables and stories in *The Book of Delight* see p. 13 in the introduction to Hadas' translation. It would also be well to point out that none of the other subordinate stories, i.e., the stories which are not animal fables, are the same as the ones in the *Libro*.

[11] Cf. Hades' translation, pp. 147–48.

the collection of Walter the Englishman.[12] The tale of the panic–
stricken hares and frogs would serve well as an illustration. The first
six verses of the model text go as follows:

> Silva sonat, fugiunt Lepores, palus obviat, herent;
> Fit mora, respiciunt ante retroque, timent.
> Dum vibrant in mente metus, se mergere pacti
> Se metui et Ranas stagna subire vident.
> Unus ait: Sperare licet; non sola timoris
> turba sumus; vano Rana timore latet; ... (vv. 1–6)

(A noise is heard in the forest and the hares flee. But the swamp
is in the way. They stop, they hesitate, they look backward and
forward anxiously. In the grip of fear they agree to huddle
together. And then they see the frogs take fright and get into the
murky water. One [of the hares] calls out: "It may be good [at
times] to wait and see. Are we just a fearful bunch? The frogs
are hiding because of an empty scare; ...)

The Archpriest for his part has this in stanzas 1445–47):

> Andávanse las liebres   en la silva allegadas;
> sonó un poco la silva,   fuxieron espantadas:
> fue sueno de laguna   e ondas rebatadas.
> Las liebres temerosas   en uno son juntadas;
>
> catan a todas partes,   non pueden quedas ser,
> dizen con el gran miedo: ¿quién se fuesse asconder?
> Ellas esto fablando   ovieron de veer
> las ranas con su miedo   so el agua meter.
>
> Dixo la una liebre: "Conviene que esperemos:
> non somos nos señeras   que miedo vano avemos,

---

[12] Cf. Lecoy, pp. 136–37. For the complete text of Walter's fables see L.
Hervieux, *Les Fabulistes latins*, vol. 2., pp. 316–51 (the passage cited in the
text appears on pp. 329–30). Numerous other examples of the close
correspondence between Walter and the Spanish poet could be given.

> las ranas se asconden   de balde, ya lo vemos:
> las liebres e las ranas   vano temor tenemos;

Our poet even reproduces to some extent Walter's diction with Castilian derivatives. One would search to no avail in Lida's studies for an indication of a similarity between the *Libro* and *The Book of Delight* as close as this.[13]

Which brings us to the heart of the matter: A radical proposal like that of Lida must perforce rest on some hard evidence.[14] If there is no reference in the Archpriest's poem to one of the Hebrew source authors or their works (nor an instance of a close textual dependency) then, at the least, a reference to any other Jewish writing would help (discounting, of course, banalities and the documents revered by Christians and Jews alike). But even this much is not forthcoming in the *Libro*. On the other hand references to Western Latin writings abound.

How was the Archpriest able to acquire knowledge of several works of Hebrew literature? Did he know the language? In no uncertain terms Lida advocates an indirect familiarity, and points to stanza 1513 as evidence that our poet was well disposed to Spanish Jews.[15] The passage goes as follows:

> Después muchas cantigas   fiz de dança e troteras
> para judías e moras   e para entenderas;
> para en estrumentes,   comunales maneras:
> el cantar que non sabes,   oílo a cantaderas.

Needless to say, verses *ab* (the ones which count and then only in part) convey no sure indication that the author was familiar with Hebrew since the everyday parlance of the Jews was in *romance*.

---

[13] For another instance of a source text not identified by the poet one might cite the *Ordo commendationis animae* (a formal ecclesiastical supplication) which is patently the basis for *Libro* stanzas 1–7. The *Poema de Fernán González* also contains a version (sts. 105–13).

[14] This is not to say that Lida's correspondences lack totally for relevance. The question is simply: to what extent do they carry weight?

[15] *Estud. de lit.*, pp. 24–25.

Nor need the verses indicate that he felt attracted to the Jews to a greater degree than any other juglar who composed compositions for public festivals.[16] He was simply ready and able to provide entertainment for the general run of Castilians. He was also ready and able to refer to his own creations.

Indeed, there is reason to believe he was personally supportive of the anti–Semitism of his day, a bias which would seemingly have caused him to keep his distance from Jewish religious practice and intellectual activity. At the beginning of the *Libro* in stanza one, verses *ab* we read:

> Señor Dios, que a los judíos,   pueblo de perdición,
> saqueste de cativo   del poder de Faraón,

Lida sets down this notion of "pueblo de perdición" as "solemnidad de portada."[17] But there is more to come farther down in the poem.

----

[16] If the stanza is indicative of an interest in Hebrew literature, that is not evident. The poet's concern with Jewish and Moorish women seems to relate rather to a jamboree of *juglares* (cf. Menéndez Pidal, pp. 98–99). On p. 25 of *Estud. de lit.* Lida cites *Libro* 78d, 554c, 1183–84, 1212b as revealing "huellas" of the poet's familiarity with Jews. And yet the information concerning Jews in these verses is meager and banal. Looking, for example, at all of 554 we read:

> "Non quieras jugar dados   nin seas tablajero,
> ca es mala ganancia,   peor que de logrero:
> el judío al año   da tres por quatro, pero
> el tablax de un día   dobla el su mal dinero."

There was legislation in Castile at the time which put a cap on the amount of interest Jews could charge for a loan. The statement in verse *c* could easily be nothing more than a reference to this sort of restriction. The full sense of 554cd, for that matter, is not without an element of resentment. The idea seems to be that a gambling hustler can rake in even more profit than a Jewish lender, i.e., someone thought to make excessive monetary demands. In 554c one encounters in a small way the perennial European motif of the "shylock."

[17] *Dos obras*, p. 20. The only other comment on the nature of the poet's

In stanza 1053 we read as follows concerning the injustice done to Christ:

> A la tercia ora
> Cristos fue juzgado:
> juzgólo el Atora,
> pueblo porfiado:
> por aquesto mora
> en cativo dado,
> del qual nunca saldrá
> nin avrá librador.

And in 1063:

> Por salvar fue venido
> el linaje umanal;
> fue de Judas vendido
> por muy poco cabal;
> fue preso e ferido
> de los judíos muy mal:
> est Dios, en que creemos,
> fuéronlo açotar;

The reference is again, of course, to Christ. And at length in 1657 we have:

> El Señor de Paraíso

---

anti–Semitism occurs on p. 25 in *Estud. de lit.* where we find the statement "...la actitud convencional hacia los judíos exhibida cuando el poeta ahueca la voz..." But given her proposal Lida should properly have more to say. What she does, in effect, is gloss over at full speed various passages highly damaging to her thesis. All in all, the best one can conclude about the poet's view of Jews is that in the sphere of public interaction his hostility was restrained. For a strongly hostile stance one might consider the mob violence presented by Gonzalo de Berceo in a positive light (sts. 371–72 and 426–29 of the *Milagros*). Our Archpriest was not so radical. Still, here and there, the *Libro* reveals a degree of enmity.

a cristianos tanto quiso
que por nos la muerte priso:
matáronlo los judíos;

The Jews as pertinacious Christ tormentors and killers! Our poet was quite conscious of the meaning of "pueblo de perdición" and did not fail to bring it out. That he should seek then in the very same work to imitate rabbinical literature seems unlikely. This consideration alone is enough to render Lida's case for a dependency of the *Libro* on three Hebrew books suspect.

On the other hand in the Pseudo–Ovidian *De vetula* we have a viable alternative to the works proposed by Castro and Lida.[18] Like the *Libro* the poem comprises a large number of thematically heterogeneous pieces including —to mention only those having a specific counterpart in the Spanish composition—: a statement concerning the effects of love (Book I, vv. 1–51), a statement concerning musical instruments (I, 64–70), a reference to a decorated wall said to contain an inner meaning (I, 92–97), a criticism of games of chance (I, 358–576), a satire directed at the legal profession (I, 737–65), a complaint against the power of money (I, 766–810), a description of an ideal female type (II, 243–36), a description of a grotesque female type (II, 500–08), a prisoner's lament (III, 439–50), an astrological development (III, 451–643), and a prayer to the Virgin Mary (III, 772–811: presented within the context of a pretended prophecy).[19]

Many of these similarities were first pointed out by Francisco Rico in an article published in 1967.[20] But the principal overall affinity between the *De vetula* and the *Libro* —here too, an affinity pointed out by Rico— consists of an autobiographic pretense which

---

[18] As already noted all references to the *De vetula* correspond to the edition of Klopsch (the work is divided, as one may recall, into three sections or "Books").

[19] In a recent study John Dagenais describes the overall thematic character of the *Libro* as "a vast intertextual web" (*The Ethics of Reading in Manuscript Culture*, p. 142). A felicitous designation.

[20] See his article "Sobre el origen de la autobiografía en el *Libro de buen amor*."

extends throughout the two compositions and serves to bind together the potpourri of subordinate themes. The autobiography in itself, however, represents only part of the similarity: also apparent is that this proffered personal history comes especially to the fore in a central episode, an episode which is amatory in theme and takes up the longest single extension of verse in the poem.

In question with respect to the *Libro* is the "Endrina," our well–known story of how the Archpriest was able to violate an attractive woman with the help of a go–between. The counterpart in the *De vetula*, however, is little known, and it would be well to summarize the plot.

At the start "Ovid" draws up a description of an ideal female type which, as he informs us, depicts his ladylove.[21] But he was unable to approach her, we are told, because of the protection afforded by her parents. So he decided to persuade a certain old woman, i.e., *vetula*, to act as go–between. To get the latter to consent was not easy: he had to haggle a good deal over payment. Finally she agreed and set about the task. After an extensive wait the old woman informed him that she had made the arrangements: he was to come to the lady's house at night and pass through a certain door into a chamber; there he would find his beloved in bed and could take his pleasure. He did as bidden, but alas, once in bed, found himself embracing not his lady, but the go–between herself! He returned home filled with resentment and railed in anger at the trickster. Nonetheless, he eventually went on to possess his beloved. That, however, did not occur until many years later when she too had become something of a *vetula*. True satisfaction, therefore, was not to be his. He began, accordingly, to turn from the pursuit of sexual love, and devote himself to philosophic and religious inquiry (an account of which follows thereafter in Book Three).

Evident from the preceding —an important factor overlooked by Rico— is that the reader is face to face in Book Two with a reworking of the *Pamphilus*, so retold as to constitute a pivotal event in "Ovid's" autobiography. And likewise is it with the

---

[21] The piece is nothing other than a *descriptio pulcritudinis feminæ* (see above p. 24-5).

"Endrina Adventure" in the *Libro*: the poet has made use of the same source so as to create a key event in the love life of his "I" narrator.

Here, then, in the *De vetula* is a similarity to the *Libro* in both structure and theme which easily outdoes the semitic proposals set forth as a model for the Archpriest's poem. Indeed, the procedure in the *Libro* is not restricted to the "Endrina": as indicated previously, adaptations of the *Pamphilus* woven into the autobiography turn up repeatedly in the *Libro*. Our poet has made extensive use of the *Pamphilus* for his pretended personal history.

And there is more: prior to the "Endrina" one comes across several incidental ideas relative to the amatory plot which may stem from the *De vetula*. In stanzas 438 and 439 we read as follows concerning the appropriate type of old woman to be engaged as an intermediary:

> Si parienta non tienes   atal, toma unas viejas
> que andan las iglesias   e saben las callejas:
> grandes cuentas al cuello,   saben muchas consejas;
> con lágrimas de Moisén   escantan las orejas;
>
> grandes maestras son   aquestas paviotas:
> andan por todo el mundo,   por plaças e por cotas,
> a Dios alçan las cuentas,   querellando sus coitas:
> ¡Ai quánto mal saben   estas viejas arlotas!

The verses occur in the *ars amandi* recited by the love god don Amor to the lovelorn Archpriest (sts 423–575, i.e., in the episode immediately preceding the "Endrina"). We know, of course, that the lover–protagonist will go on in the "Endrina" to fulfill his sexual ambition with the help of just such a go–between. But what is the source of the go–between's type? Of interest here is not that she is an old woman (a characteristic obviously necessary for continuity), but that she is given to religious ostentation. The *Pamphilus* itself says nothing in this respect; the most we are told is in verses 281–84 which conveys the protagonist's intent to seek an intermediary:[22]

> Hic prope degit anus subtilis et ingeniosa
>   Artibus et Veneris apta ministra satis.
> Postpositis curis ad eam vestigia vertam
>   et sibi consilium notifcabo meum. (vv. 281–84)

(There's a smart, quick talking old woman who lives near here;
she knows quite well how to be of use in matters of love. So I'll
just stop worrying, go find her, and let her know what's on my
mind.)

If we turn, however, to the equivalent event in the *De vetula* we
find that the narrator has this to say in connection with his need for
a go–between:

> Talia cum vigili cura meditarer apud me
> totque revolvissem vetulas et sepe diuque
> singula librassem lustrans urbem spatiosam,
> occurrit tandem, quod erat paupercula quedam
> linguipotensque, mee vicina sororis, apud quam
> sæpe dabatur ei cibus intuitu pietatis,
> et fuerat quondam dilecte sedula nutrix. (II, vv. 355–61)

(While I was giving careful thought to these things, looking
about the metropolis, evaluating many old women, and considering often and at length one thing after another, it happened
that a certain poor old woman with a gift for gab turned up; she
was a neighbor of my sister and frequently received something
to eat in her house because of her pious appearance. In addition,
she had once been my lady's devoted nursemaid.)

We need not think that the entire description of the Archpriest's
intermediary had a written source: much of it may have come from
personal experience and artistic imagination. Nonetheless one may

---

[22] The quotation is from the edition of Becker.

well wonder: was this "pius appearance" of the go–between in the
De vetula the point of departure for the attribution of religious
fakery to the go–between in the *Libro*?

Another *Libro* passage possibly based (one is tempted to say
probably based) on the *De vetula* is stanza 527 where don Amor
gives the lover a piece of advice relative to his dealings with the
go–between:

> Guárdate non te abuelvas a la casamentera:
> doñear non la quieras, ca es una manera
> por que t' farié perder a la entendedera:
> ca una conlueça de otra siempre tiene dentera.

As mentioned previously, Felix Lecoy described these verses as
a "survival," i.e., an unsuitable carryover from Ovid's *Ars amatoria*
where at one point (Book I, vv. 375–98) the lover is advised not to
seduce his lady's handmaid.[23] But this position is open to question.
The Archpriest's go–between is an old woman while the age of the
Roman poet's handmaid is left undefined. Are we to assume that
she too is an old woman? In any case, the *Libro* intermediary has
almost nothing in common with the handmaid in the *Ars*. Above
all, she is not the beloved's servant (as stipulated by the love god in
st. 436). If we adhere, then, to Lecoy we are required to assume that
our poet: 1) ignored or forgot the type of his own intermediary, and
2) in a sudden isolated stanza went on to bring in advice from the
Ars which for the *Libro* was now distinctly incongruous. The French
scholar's explanation amounts to an assumption based on an
assumption.

On the other hand, with one stroke the problem of stanza 527
is resolved if we interpret the passage in the light of the *De vetula*.
All one need do is take the sense as an ironic allusion made en
passant to the sexual farce in the pseudo–Ovidian poem. And this
approach has more than just simplicity to speak for it: on balance
the evidence that our poet knew the imitative work is as great, if

---

[23] *Recherches*, p. 305.

not greater, than the evidence for his having known a true composition of Ovid.

The similarity of the *Libro* to the *De vetula* is too striking to be set aside. Among other affinities both works contain an adaptation of the *Pamphilus* serving as a pivotal event in a pretended autobiography. It seems likely, therefore, that the Archpriest had knowledge of the 13th–century composition. But what kind of knowledge? Did he read the poem directly? Or did he read about it (or simply hear about it)? A fair response has to incline to the latter possibility: as of yet, one can point to nothing definite in favor of a direct familiarity. There is however a certainty: all the model texts that have contributed indisputably to the formation of the *Libro* derive from the Western Latin legacy. And so too does the *De vetula*: the poem stands squarely in the tradition of imitative Ovidiana.

It would be impossible to say as much for Castro's and Lida's Semitic proposals: both scholars were not only obliged to posit an indirect knowledge on the part of the Archpriest, but were also obliged to offer gratuitous assertions as to how he was able to acquire that knowledge (especially Lida who fails to take the poet's anti–Semitism justly into account). One does better closer to home: in view of the existence of the *De vetula*, the Arabizing and Judaizing contentions —never bolstered by hard evidence— seem superfluous.

VI
In Summary

FOR MUCH OF THE 20th century *Libro* scholars have inclined to assume that the poetry of Ovid played a role in the formation of the Spanish masterpiece. And indeed, an Ovidian presence of a sort is undeniable. But two questions perforce arise, questions which have never been fully discussed. To wit: in what way did the Archpriest have knowledge of the Roman poet's verse, and to what extent did he make use of it in his own creation?

One can understand why comparatively little has been written in this respect: a lack of useful editions of the relevant poetry. Not that modern versions of the authentic works of Ovid have been unavailable: these have existed aplenty, especially since the 19th century. The same cannot be said, however, for the imitative verse which had an impact, if only indirectly, on the Archpriest's inspiration. Among the pertinent compositions a workable edition of the *De amore* appeared in the 1890s. For the *Pamphilus* however not much of value appeared until the 1930s, and for the *Pseudo–Ars amatoria* and the pseudo–Ovidian *De vetula* even less until the 1960s.

The extent to which the Archpriest drew upon such pieces varies. On the one hand there can be no doubt he incorporated into the *Libro* a Spanish rendition of virtually the entire *Pamphilus*. At a certain point, for that matter, he formally acknowledges this "elegiac comedy" as his model. On the other hand, there is reason to think he did not know and use the verse of Ovid himself. In several places he speaks of the Roman poet as his source, but does so with reference to something of medieval origin. Also, most of the *Libro* passages one might possibly consider drawn from the *Ars amatoria* (the only truly viable work) prove upon further examination to be adapted from an imitative poem. The remaining passages comprise a few snippets and are just as dissimilar as similar to a supposed counterpart in the antique model. All in all, hard evidence that the Castilian poet made direct use of Ovid's guide to seduction is lacking.

Though written in prose, the *De amore* of Andreas Capellanus demonstrates many characteristics of imitative Ovidian literature. Especially noteworthy is the juxtaposition of two seemingly contradictory themes: a promotion of profligate sexual behavior side by side with a condemnation of all human sexuality; no serious attempt is made to reconcile the one with the other: they simply coexist.

Something analogous occurs over a certain portion of the *Libro*. For 241 stanzas the reader learns of the wicked depredations caused by sexual love. Nonetheless, in the 152 stanzas which come thereafter a lesson in the art of seduction is imparted as if nothing to the contrary had been previously stated. The similarity to the *De amore* is striking. One would be hard put however to show a direct dependency. The affinity probably results from nothing more than a common outlook in the imitative tradition: a lascivious composition was thought to have a greater chance of survival if accompanied by a palliative. That there be a logical or consequential relationship mattered little.

The *Pseudo–Ars amatoria*, for its part, had a direct impact on the *Libro*. Much of don Amor's instruction in love can be traced to this 12th century(?) *ars amandi*. Various segments of his lesson represent, in fact, a fairly literal rendition of the source equivalent. But the Archpriest made use of the *Pseudo–Ars* not only for pieces of advice: evident as well is that his adaptations create a thematic framework allowing for the inclusion of miscellaneous subtopics into the Spanish poem. One might mention the "Enxiemplo de la propiedat qu'el dinero ha," a stock theme with only partial relevance to the surrounding context. Don Amor's discourse appears to have been employed as a catchall for compositions that were probably preexistent.

A *Libro* source that would not fail to be recognized as such in the Archpriest's day is the ever popular *Pamphilus*. The story (related in dramatic dialog) tells how a lover achieved a seduction with the help of an unscrupulous old woman. The latter, acting as go–between, eventually maneuvered the beloved into a situation where she could be violated with impunity. And yet there is an open–ended hint at an ethical ending: in her final speech the go–between suggests the lover and his lady get married.

The Archpriest offers his reader a mostly faithful rendition of the source. But he also introduces some modifications and additions. Especially conspicuous are his comments by way of epilog. Here he seeks to justify the existence of the Spanish version with a manifold palliative (including a decisive affirmation in retrospect that the lover and his lady got married). His efforts proved, however, to little avail: the text of the story as we have it has been brutally bowdlerized. What was permissible in an academic language was not permissible in a vernacular.

The existence of the pseudo–Ovidian *De vetula* (mid–13th century) would seem to indicate there was a precedent for the overall thematic type of the *Libro*. The two compositions have a good deal in common. Both contain an autobiographic narrative (stressing the amatory aspect) which runs the length of the work and provides a unifying context for subordinate topics. Also both contain a version of the *Pamphilus* so redone as to constitute a cardinal event in the life of the narrator. The similarity is patent.

Nonetheless one cannot say the *Libro* reveals a direct dependency on the *De vetula*. Apparently the Archpriest only read about the pseudo–Ovidian poem. Or perhaps he only heard about it. Such could easily have occurred: the large number of manuscripts which have survived (more than 30) implies the work was well known during the late Middle Ages. In any case this much is certain: our Spanish bard made use of other pieces of imitative Ovidiana; that he should make use of the *De vetula* as well need come as no surprise.

APPENDICES
Translations of the *Pamphilus*, the *Pseudo-ars Amatoria*, and Verses 202-728 in Book Two of the *De Vetula*

INCLUDED AS APPENDICES are English versions of the *Pamphilus* and the *Pseudo-Ars amatoria*, the Neo-Latin poems which underlie two of the principal episodes in the *Libro de buen amor*. Also included is a version of the central event in the pseudo-Ovidian *De vetula*. The texts used are those of Becker, Thiel, and Klopsch respectively (see BIBLIOGRAPHY for specifics). The translations represent an attempt to make use of contemporary American English while at the same time keeping as closely as possible to the sense of the original. No easy task, admittedly. But perhaps someone will find the result useful.

APPENDIX A:
The *Pamphilus*

PAMPHILUS ALONE:

I've been struck by a dart and I carry it deep in my heart. Though the wound and the pain grow constantly I cannot say the name of my assailant and the injury itself is invisible. What's more, I see that future dangers will bring greater harm. I simply have no hope for recovery. How can I deal with this problem? It's terrible. What am I going to do? I wander about in confusion. I want to complain and I've good reason to do so since I'm at a total loss for help. There's so much that is harmful; I'll have to be careful. The smart individual can always come through. If my wound were to reveal itself, what it is like, where it comes from, who made the attack, I could lose all hope of recovery. Hope can restore a confident person, but it can also deceive him. If my wound were to conceal its nature and its pain, and I never looked for a chance of a cure, things would get worse and worse, and eventually I would have to die. I consider it better, therefore, to acknowledge what has happened. A blaze that's concealed can be something fierce; but if it's exposed, it's generally less destructive. And so I'll speak to Venus; she is our life and our death; everything is subject to her decisions.

Sole hope of every living thing, Venus known to all, hail to you! You who force all to submit to your rule, you whom powerful dukes and kings fear and serve, in your kindness take pity on my humble petition. Don't be hard with me, don't refuse my request. Please do as I ask; what I want is not much. I just said it's not much, and yet to someone miserable like me it seems like a great deal. But for you to accede is not hard at all. Say only: "I grant it," and right away I'll be in ecstasy and all will turn out well.

There's a young woman who lives close by (I wish she did not, but let it be so, if you will only come to my aid). As you know, a blaze up close is usually more harmful than one that is far off. Just so, this neighbor would hurt less if she were far away. People talk about her and say she's more beautiful than any one else in our part of town. Either I'm deceived by love, or she really does surpass them all. She has pierced my heart with an accurate shot, a shot I myself am unable to remove. From hour to hour the pain of the wound increases, while my healthy complexion, my strength, my attractiveness all diminish. I have not spoken of this to anyone, I have not said who caused my wound. But then again it's only proper that nothing be said. People talk about her and say —I admit it's the truth— that she is born into a social class higher than mine; that's why I'm afraid to speak to her of my desire. They also say, and again it's true, that she's quite rich, and where there's wealth there's a need for propriety and marriage with a dowry. I have no distinction, no resources, no great means. Whatever I manage to get, I get on my own. Yes, the daughter of a farmer, provided that she's rich, can have her pick from thousands of men. At the very sight of her I get a sensation all over my body, and this too, keeps me from telling her of my devotion. A woman who feels assured of her beauty easily becomes conceited and dispenses with a need to show restraint. I have tried to cleanse my heart of this longing, but the more I resist the more I burn with love. You know how it is, you see what I'm going through, you see my plight. All I ask is that you deal kindly with my request. But you refuse to give me an answer or lend an ear to what I say or to look at me. Pluck your arrows from my heart; do something to relieve my awful wound. Who can put up with an inner turmoil that leads to nothing and always causes tears? I have no choice but to beg of you. My constant pain wears me down and forces me to implore you again and again. (vv. 1–70)

VENUS:
Then Venus said this:[1] A constant effort will win out. If you

---

[1] Then Venus said this ("Tunc Venus hec inquit"), the only statement in the *Pamphilus* not within dramatic discourse.

only make an effort you will enjoy any woman you want. Do not hesitate to demonstrate your feelings; there is hardly one woman in a thousand who will turn you down. The woman you are pursuing may at first be harsh and say no, but her harshness means very little. As you are aware, what the vendor swears at first is not for sale, the insistent buyer will soon have as his own. Likewise no sailor would get across the sea if he took fright at the first big wave that bumped against his ship. Therefore, if at first a woman shows no interest when you talk to her, see to it that she becomes more responsive by means of your skill, by means of your know–how. Skillfulness can break the will to resist, it can overthrow strong cities. With skill towers can be reduced, heavy loads carried off; with skill fish can be caught from under the waves and a man can traverse the sea without getting wet. Skill and know–how are useful in many situations: by means of know–how a poor person is often able to feed himself; another person can placate the anger of a prince, even though his anger is right and just; the criminal is able to keep himself from harm and retain his loot; he who once wept in his poverty can rejoice in his wealth; and he who once went on foot goes later on horseback. The man who got nothing from his parents, if he can make use of his skill, will presently have something.

If at first she should reject your attentions, go ahead and serve her anyway. In this way you will overcome the obstacles she will place in your way. She who was once hostile will become your friend. Go often to those places where she can usually be found. If you can, amuse her with wittiness; young people like to have fun and indulge in light conversation; such things put them into an amorous mood. And always show her a cheerful face! Every man is more handsome when he is cheerful. Do not be too silent on the one hand and do not say what is needless on the other; a young woman often dislikes a man for the slightest of reasons. An abundance of sweet talk incites and promotes a feeling of love; by using a little flattery you can soften a hard disposition. If the circumstance is suitable, be insistent in a playful but forceful way. What you hardly hoped for she herself will presently give you. Modesty will sometimes keep her from yielding to her passion; she would prefer to reject what she actually desires; she considers it better to lose her virginity under force than to say simply: "Do with me as you want."

Above all, if your means are meager, see that she does not know about your poverty and how little you possess. Ingenuity can turn an indigent life into a decent one. So conceal your tears behind a happy face. With your speech and your manners you can pretend to be what you are not. With just a bit of cleverness you can suddenly come upon good fortune. There is a much that goes on in this world of which people in general are unaware; they could be informed of much that they should know. Believe me, people often find it useful to lie. Telling the truth, for that matter, can even do harm on occasion! And so with friendly conversation and the giving of gifts gain the confidence of her household servants, both the men and the women, especially those who often talk to her, so that they, each in turn, may always speak well of you. Have them "feed" your lady with your praises! And then, when she hesitates and is unable to make up her mind —undecided whether to yield to your passion or not— you should constantly attack and entice so that you can end up the victor and enjoy her love. Once in a state of indecision a person's will can be driven hither and thither at the slightest impulse.

The two of you should always have a go–between, someone who can do a shrewd job telling each one what he or she wants (to hear). Jealous old people, as you know, pass judgement on the activities of the young and in a spirit of resentment prevent them from talking to each other.

Well then, get busy! Things have gone well in the past, and will continue to go well in the future. It's just a matter of time and some optimism. And stop being afraid of situations that make you anxious. I shall say no more. If you apply yourself, you will win your lady's love. Just make a start and a thousand possibilities will come your way. (71–142)

PAMPHILUS ALONE:

It's easy for someone who has never had an injury to give advice to someone who has been seriously hurt. And yet that same injured person continues to feel the presence of his pain. My suffering has not been relieved by Venus' advice. On the contrary, these pangs of love are still tormenting my heart. Up till now I have put my hope in her, and now my hope is fading and my suffering persists. I can't escape from this misery. I've been abandoned at sea in search of a haven I'm unable to find. What am I going to do? My only hope depends on the girl, and as luck would have it I'm about to get an opportunity to talk to her. Here she comes, and oh, how beautiful she is with her hair unbound! Here is the chance, if ever there was one, to talk to her! But suddenly I'm overcome by fears and more fears: I've lost my reason and my ability to speak, my energy is gone, my hands and my feet are trembling; my usual self is in a state of shock. I have so much stored up in me which I'm ready to tell her. But this fearfulness makes me want to give up what I intended to do. I'm not the person I was; I hardly know myself; I can hardly control what I have to say. But I'll go ahead and speak to her anyway. (143–62)

PAMPHILUS TO GALATHEA:

My niece from the town nearby wants me to greet you cordially on her behalf and offer you her services. She knows you only by name and from what she has heard of you. But if it were possible, she would like to meet you personally. My kinsmen (who are numerous in that place and make up the upper crust) wanted to get me to stay there. They promised me a girl with a big dowry and a lot of other things which I shall not bother to mention. I ignored it all. It's you alone whom I like. For you I would reject everything in the world. We speak lightly; that's the way young people talk to each other. Easy conversation doesn't cause any trouble. But let us now tell each other our secrets from the heart. No one can know what we have to say. Let us give a pledge! I'll speak. I started first, so I'll speak first.

First of all, we should be in complete agreement to speak the truth. There is no other person in the world I like more than you. Three years have passed during which I have loved you and did not dare to mention my desire. It is surely unwise to speak at length to a deaf person, and we too should obviously not speak in vain to each other. I love you, that's all. I shall say no more until you, for your part, say what you think of me. (163–86)

GALATHEA:

That's the way many men entice and deceive young women. That's the kind of deceitful offer with which many women are led into a trap. You thought you could make an imbecile of me with your smooth talk and tricks. But I'm not one of those who can be taken in with your falsehood. Your kind should chase after some tramp or other; they're the ones you can make fools of with your trickery and your empty loyalty. (187–92)

PAMPHILUS:

It often happens that good men are frustrated by the wrongs done by bad men. You shouldn't blame me for the faults of someone else. But please, do have the kindness to listen to me and understand. You really should allow me to say a few things, my dearest. I swear to the God of Heaven and to the spirits of the earth that I speak without fraud or deception. No woman in all the world is finer than you. No woman I have ever seen or known is dearer to my heart than you. But I speak to no avail: even though we young people are usually more perceptive than our elders —believe me, old men see many things, but the young see more— with your innocence and youth you can not really be aware of what is harmful and what is good. And yet, though you are young, you should at least be able to know me for what I am, and how I love you. Knowledge of the world around us increases with experience. Yes, experience and sound instruction provide the wisdom common to human beings. I beg you only to allow that I may come and go and that we may converse. We can't get to know what we really think except by conversation. Why don't you tell me now what you think? (193–212)

GALATHEA:

I'm not preventing you or anyone from coming, going, or talking. Everyone who walks on the streets has a right to do so and to go where he wants. It's right and proper that a girl should give an answer to someone who asks her a question, or that she address a person she happens to notice. I do not object to you —or anyone else— approaching me, provided only you do nothing to offend me. It's permissible for a girl to listen and reply. But there is also a matter of going too far. If your intention is to make light conversation, I too will engage in light conversation. But if what you have to say is offensive, that I will not allow. You ask for a get-together; I want nothing to do with getting together alone. It is not proper for us to be by ourselves somewhere. A meeting like that can be risky; that's the way a bad reputation starts up. I'll speak to you only in a safe place in view of other people. (213–26)

PAMPHILUS:

It's nothing small, but a great boon you have granted. All I ever wanted, you know, was to talk to you. I don't know how I can show an appreciation worthy of the benefit you have given me. No words are capable of doing justice to this concession. But perhaps the day and the time will yet come when you will see how much of a friend I am. I hope it doesn't upset you, I hardly dare to come out with it although I have obviously asked you for very little up till now. But if there were a chance, could we embrace and kiss and touch each other? (227–36)

GALATHEA:

An embrace can lead to a forbidden love affair, and the woman who gives kisses is often deceived by them. But I shall say yes, provided, of course, that you try to get nothing more. I would not permit this to anyone other than you. But look over there: both my parents are coming back after attending worship. To avoid unpleasantry it would be better for me to go home now. There will be lots of time later for us to talk. In the meantime each of us can think of the other. (237–44)

PAMPHILUS ALONE:

There's no happier man in the world than I and there never was one. My anchor has taken hold. All of a sudden God and good fortune have blessed me. I who was once poor went out and came back rich. Did she really ask me to think about her? Try as I might, I can hardly get her out of my mind! She doesn't feel the way I do; she doesn't know how much I want her. Yes, let her have me on her mind just as I have her on my mind! Well then, I'm free from one set of predicaments. But others I don't know how to deal with continue to oppress me. If I become too eager, and chat and joke

with her too often, talk and gossip will make their usual rounds. On
the other hand, if I don't keep on with the chase so that we get
closer, her love for me, which is still not very strong, will fade.
Familiarity causes love to grow, lack of contact causes it to
diminish. A love that is not kept nourished will soon grow weak. A
fire that is constantly fed with wood will surge. But if you take
away the wood, it will quickly go out. I'm upset, torn back and forth
by so many worries, risks, possibilities. I'm at a loss as to what to
do. I still don't see any chance of success in this affair. I can't think
of any way to keep going. And there is also Lady Fortune who
stands in the way: she allows no leeway for what men may want to
do. To many men she causes harm, to many others she gives a
blessing. That's the way we live in this world. It's God and our own
actions which reward and provide for us. Here on earth nothing but
God and our own efforts count for something. May He, then, be the
guardian and director of all my undertakings. May He govern all
that I do and intend to do.

As a go–between I won't use my brother or nephew. You simply
can't have confidence in that sort of person. When it comes to the
madness of love neither a brother nor a nephew has any loyalty or
honor. The slightest thing can cause trouble and the smart person
avoids what is harmful. It would be best, therefore, to make other
arrangements.

There's a smart, quick talking old woman who lives near hear;
she knows quite well how to be of use in matters of love. So I'll just
stop worrying, go find her, and let her know what's on my mind.
(245–84)

PAMPHILUS TO OLD WOMAN:

I've heard people sing your praises and speak of your quality.
And so I have come to you for advice. I beg of you, Madame, please
listen to what I have to say and don't mention it to anyone else
without my approval. There's a neighbor of mine whom I love;
Galathea is her name (I think you know her). Unless I'm mistaken
she loves me too, at least that's what she says. I can't speak to her
as I would like to; it's much too risky. I get anxious and all upset
about some mishap or other that could occur. A rumor can start up
from a trivial matter and take a long time to die down. Even if the

rumor is a lie, it still spreads all around. Trifling things do harm to the lowly; a thousand problems plague the poor. Whatever they undertake has no sure outcome. You can see the difficulties we have to face. And so I would like you to act as an intermediary between the two of us. I only ask that you conceal what we are up to in your comings and goings. (285–98)

OLD WOMAN:

Someone else loves the woman you do, and what you want is what he wants too. But he doesn't have my support. He's got "class," and is good enough to have a decent wife. But I don't like the way he tried to pay me. He promised some old clothes along with a leather piece. His cheap reward did him out of my help. A suitable payment, made on time, can have a lot of effect. With a little bit of ingenuity it's easy to get around the rules. No one, I think, is going to have this woman you're after except through me; she's completely under my control. In fact, she looks to me for direction; she lets me know what she does; she acts only on my advice. I can't talk now any longer; I have to see to something else. Everybody should make his own way and watch out for himself. (299–312)

PAMPHILUS:

This affaire means everything to me; nothing else is of consequence. If you can deliver this woman to me you will have done a fine job. It's often appropriate that we engage the services of others and also appropriate that the work they do be properly rewarded. In no sense, believe me, will you have done a job without a reward if you can only get me what I long for. I ask just this: tell me what I can pay you. Whatever you say, I'll give it. (313–20)

OLD WOMAN:

People who suffer from poverty seek and ask for a lot. I'm ashamed to tell you how much I need. I was well–to–do when I was in my prime. But my wealth is gone, I need so many things. My age and weakness have stripped me clean; my talents and hard work provide no comfort for me. If you think I can help you, then I ask that from now on you open your house to me. (321–28)

PAMPHILUS:

From this point on my house and everything I have will be at your disposal; all I possess is yours to manage. We are now bound by an agreement which I find quite acceptable. May the pact and the trust that goes with it act to encourage us. But I would ask this: that you make a true genuine effort. Use your wits to see that the affaire turns out well. A careful approach involves giving thought to both the beginning and the end of a matter; the outcome determines whether what was done was shameful or honorable. Take care as to how you will begin to speak, and how you will finish; if you have thought about what you're going to say, your words will come out better. (329–38)

OLD WOMAN (NO LONGER WITH PAMPHILUS AND PRETENDING NOT TO NOTICE THE PRESENCE OF GALATHEA):

What fine young people there are in this town! What a growth in every good habit and custom. In my time there was no one better or nicer than he; he's going to do something for me in my need. He stands out among his peers for his kindness, he outdoes his companions in worth. He deals simply with the simple and is as gentle as a lamb with the gentle. But still, wise person that he is, he doesn't put up with any foolishness. There's just no young man who can match him in this city. The money he has he does not use up in eating and drinking. He's just so decent. And then too, he comes from a good family: from a sweet tree falls a sweet piece of fruit. Mother Nature frequently tells you something about the family by way of the children; a son is usually like his father. But what's this? Do I see Galathea at the door? Could it be she heard what I said? (339–54)

OLD WOMAN TO GALATHEA:

I didn't think anyone was nearby, Galathea. And yet what I was saying is very true. Pamphilus surely outdoes everyone around town. The life he leads is really good. People mention him more and more, speak highly of him, praise him. And no one begrudges him for what he is. He's quite rich, but he doesn't go about putting on airs. And the money he's got is "honest" money too. I wish, Galathea, that he were your husband. You too would want the same thing if you really understood this sort of business. I was only saying what I would want for you, not something he asked me to mention. As I see it, the two of you should get together: the family background, the personal quality, the good looks you have in common, all tell me you ought to be together. But I'm just dealing in idle thoughts and empty words. Still, at times a trivial matter can lead to bigger things: from a tiny spark comes a hugh fire; from a small beginning a great big result. I'm only giving thought now to the way things start. I wanted to amuse you a bit. But if you're interested in what I'm talking about, if you like the idea —or maybe you're annoyed by it?— please say so. Whatever you say I will not repeat, if you want me to keep it to myself. Or, if you want me to pass it on, I'll do so. So speak up, don't hold back, get rid of this silly modesty. Modesty only suits people who have no refinement. (355–80)

GALATHEA:

I don't lack refinement nor am I held back by silly modesty. I'm simply astonished at what you have to say. I wonder if you just happened to come along here, or if Pamphilus put you up to it, and you expect to get paid for your little speech. (381–84)

OLD WOMAN:

The wrongs that bad men do always get in the way of the actions of good men. People often have to pay a penalty they don't deserve. I'm poor, it's true, but I don't look for that kind of payment. I'm content to live with the little I have. As I said to you before, my talking was all just some thoughts I had. You know better: no one else is aware of anything. But if you would like to get together, that can easily be arranged. Each of you could do it without having to feel shame. He's of good stock, and you are too. I'm quite familiar with the background of both of you. He's more handsome than his buddies and you're better looking than your girlfriends. It's fitting and nice to see people together who suit each other. The two of you with your equal wealth and age prove it. And even if word got around, approval would be the result. Since you are so much alike you have a right to get together. You have everything except love. (385–400)

GALATHEA:

What you're saying ought to be said to the persons who take care of me. Only with their approval would I decide to get married. You go talk to them first, or let this Pamphilus fellow do it; your proposal will be more to their liking that way. (401–04)

OLD WOMAN:

It's proper that you should get married with the consent of your parents. But in the meantime you should allow the fire of your love to burn freely. Venus —she's ingenious— stirs the hearts of the young. All persons who give themselves over to her learn much about their inclinations. She stirs the spirit, she gives to the generous, she hates the greedy; she chases people who are cheerful and runs away from those who are sad. Can anyone say how much devotion to Venus is worth? If you resist her, you'll always be coarse. (405–12)

GALATHEA:

A virgin soon loses her reputation by adhering to Venus. She represents a raging fury that knows no restraint. The fierce darts of Cupid inflict a serious wound. Every girl has to fear the awful seduction that follows soon after. Gossips often find fault with girls who are innocent. A malicious jealousy doesn't cease to pick at anything. I would agree with what you say if I weren't afraid for my reputation and the way people are able to talk; this is the kind of fault they harp on. (413–20)

OLD WOMAN:

In matters like these a bad reputation tends to outrun the truth. But in the end the truth wins out and rumors simply disappear. I can free you from gossip and anxiety. I know quite well how to hide the two of you and your enjoyment. I'm familiar with the practice of Venus and the skills that go with it. You'll see, I'm capable of keeping you safe. But tell me: what do you think? What shall I say to him when I see him? If you let me know beforehand, I'll be able to speak to him with more assurance. (421–28)

GALATHEA:

I hesitate to reveal to you my hidden longing. Surely you are aware that trickery and its traps are everywhere. And yet I would like to find out if you and your talk are worth anything and where I would end up if I let myself be guided by your wiles. Pamphilus himself recently asked me for my love and then and there we got together in true friendship. But keep that to yourself. Please tell it only to him. And don't start yet to speak about these things. Put him first to the test this way and that way and often. Perhaps he himself will say exactly what I have said. Now go, and please, be very careful about all of this. And whatever he says to you, let me know about it tomorrow. (429–40)

OLD WOMAN TO PAMPHILUS:

How often our hopes and efforts meet with frustration. Things are not turning out, Pamphilus, as we wanted. You called upon me much too late to help you. My talents and my efforts are of no help to you now. It's quite clear that they are getting ready for Galathea's marriage. In fact, I'm quite astonished at the arrangements that are being made at her house. I have a bunch of reasons for suspecting what is going on, even though her father and her mother are both hiding the matter. So, please, try to understand and accept what I'm telling you. Put aside what cannot be, and seek instead what is possible. (441–50)

PAMPHILUS:

What a blow this is! I suddenly feel empty, unable to move. I can hardly think or talk. Damn it and damn it again! I feel weak all over as if I were paralyzed. My expectations have done me in! The same expectations which Venus has used to take hold of me! My hopes are gone, and yet this burning passion remains. I have the feeling of being on a ship with no chance of getting into port and no place to cast anchor. Where is there relief for my turmoil? Only Galathea has the means to ease the pain. She can kill me or cure me. If I can't have her, then I don't care if I die. (451–62)

OLD WOMAN:

You jerk! What's all this raving about! What madness got hold of you! Groaning will get you nowhere. Get smart now and control that whining. Dry those tears and let's see what can be done. "Necessity is the mother of invention;" it often brings out the ingenuity in people. A man with know–how who makes an effort can get through the toughest spots. A real effort and some sharp thinking can still help. (463–70)

PAMPHILUS:

But what can we do to get through a tight jam like this? All my hope is dead; the marriage will soon take place. As long as her husband is alive she can't get together with me. It's wrong to violate the marriage bed. The trouble I've taken has come to nothing; I'm still eager for her, but no longer have the means to take action. Neither day or night will I have any peace. This futile love is going to torment me with misery forever. (471–78)

OLD WOMAN:

A great distress will often disappear quickly and suddenly, and a fierce wind that beats down on us may bring little rain. A quiet day seems especially pleasant after a long storm. People appreciate good health more after a bad illness. Come on now, take a deep breath; forget the pain, the grief, the anger. If you're sad now you will soon be joyful. Your Galathea is going to do what we want; she will be completely under our control. (479–86)

PAMPHILUS:

Like those sweet mothers who encourage their crying children to be quiet by holding out empty promises, just so, you're treating me, it seems, to a false consolation in order to rid my heart of this sorrow and pain. (487–90)

OLD WOMAN:

You're like a bird that escapes from the talons of a hawk and then stays anxious and fearful and thinks the killer is everywhere. I have no reason for lying to you. You'll see that what I said was true. (491–94)

PAMPHILUS:

If what you're telling me and what you told me is the truth, there's no longer any grief in my heart. And yet, we don't always finish a project in the way we had intended at the beginning: a chance event often brings about a change. (495–98)

OLD WOMAN:

It's not for the minds of men to know the way of the fates. Knowledge of the future is for God alone. But to despair will do harm; with a real effort you can achieve what you want. Skill and perseverance often make for many ways to do things. Our hopes and efforts tend to change suddenly. But if you can make a good start, I'm sure your chances will increase. (499–504)

PAMPHILUS:

Do you know whether she loves me or not? A person in love can hardly keep in the secrets of the heart. (505–06)

OLD WOMAN:

When I speak, she pays very close attention to what I'm saying. It's so sweet the way she takes everything in. She puts her arms around my neck, she begs me to tell her the messages you sent her. Whenever your name comes up in our talks she becomes all aglow at just the mention. And while we're enjoying the conversation she often turns pale and then blushes. If I get tired and stop talking, she urges me to talk some more. From these and other signs I recognize that she's in love. And she doesn't deny that she's attracted to you. (507–16)

PAMPHILUS:

Now, thanks to you, I can really feel my hopes are near fulfilment. With your help I'm getting a growing sense of euphoria. A job well done resolves situations that seem at times to lack for a solution. Sluggishness and indolence, on the other hand, cause many an advantage to be lost. Try to hasten whatever you're doing as much as you can. Don't allow delay or inactivity to prolong your efforts. (517–22)

OLD WOMAN:

Yes, it looks like I've managed to arrange what you want. But I'm still not sure of that promise you made me. The way a person talks and the way he really thinks are often different; many times we don't make good on our words with our actions; we use empty promises to deceive the people who work for us. When you're finally happy maybe you too won't give me anything? (523–28)

PAMPHILUS:

How atrocious it is for a rich person to cheat the poor. If I deceived you I too would lack for all honor. No, I never dealt deceptively with you or with anyone. If you cared to look into it you would find that my reputation is free of blemish. My constant good faith lends assurance to what I say. All your interests are safe with me. Don't worry about it. (529–34)

OLD WOMAN:

We common folk are afraid of being done in by the schemes of the big shots. The rights of the poor can crumble for the smallest of reasons. Everywhere loyalty has been stripped of the worth it once had. Today it's buried under a thousand different methods for wrong–doing. And yet no one can afford to take a chance against the fates. The sea can often scare you, but it may not always be dangerous. What you promised me, I'll leave it to good fortune to provide. But the nice things I promised you, you will surely get. It would be well now that I be on my way to see if I can get the girl —if she's willing— to come here and talk to you alone. I'll use my wits and see if I can arrange for the two of you to be here at the same time. If it works out, you will have to be a man. The mind and will of a lover are always changing. A short while ought to be enough to give you what you're looking for. (535–48)

OLD WOMAN TO GALATHEA:

A huge fire can hardly hide the light it gives off; and no one can hide the desires inspired by Venus. Everything that's happening to the both of you is obvious. When I think of it, I have trouble keeping back my tears. I can see very well that the two of you are not dealing the right way with your love. This business is making its own silliness known. Your secret love shows itself both in the paleness of your faces and in the sallow color of your skin. It's as if you were suffering from some serious torment. Pamphilus, that poor guy, he's just miserable all the time; he has such a hard time dealing with that stubbornness of yours. He spends his days and nights working like a fool on a field which produces no sprouts because the ground is so tough. Who, except an idiot, scatters seed on sand? Hard work is satisfying if there's a reward in the end. It's your beauty first and then what you said which have led him astray. For these two reasons he carries the wound of an unsatisfied love. You have not been the medicine for him that you promised you would be. And now his suffering is greater than the hopes he had for things to come. Now his wound needs a salve and his pain is tremendous. And you too, even though you say nothing, your own ardent love has become a burden. People who don't admit to an injury often find that an untreated wound can cause problems and even death. In the same way a hidden passion often becomes a serious hardship. But look: what is it that you want? Why don't you give some quick thought to the matter, and then tell me in so many words how you feel about this. (549–72)

GALATHEA:

Shameless Venus often assails me with her red hot darts, and now she's constantly ordering me —she's really using force— to make love. But on the other hand, modesty and fear command me to be virtuous. I just don't know what to do anymore. (573–76)

OLD WOMAN:

Get rid of your fear completely. There's no cause for fear. There is no one at all to betray you in this business. Pamphilus wants only this: that he might be yours. His efforts have no other end but this. He revealed to me so clearly the pitiless fire that controls him, when, all in tears, he said to me: "Galathea is at once both my longing and the cure for the longing. She alone can wound me and she alone can help me." The sight of his dear sweet tears drove me to cry myself. And yet deep in my heart I was happy. I realized that things were turning out as I would have wanted; I became aware that both of you were equally on fire with love. But a fire can harm you. Please, have pity on each other! Love demands that the two of you come together through my doing! (577–90)

GALATHEA:

I want what you want; nothing would be more to my liking, if only my mother and father would agree to it. It is simply not right for me to take action on my own. But even if I were willing, there would still be no occasion for it. My mother, as you know, guards me all the time. Day and night the whole household keeps an eye on me. (591–96)

OLD WOMAN:

Love will win out: it can find a way to get doors and gates unlocked; it can find a way to get past any barrier. Do away with empty fears; don't be concerned with childish worries. Sweet Love asks that you come with me. (597–600)

GALATHEA:

You are aware now of my secret thoughts; on you above all I depend for advice. Please provide me with the counsel I need. Don't feel reluctant to say what I should do. It's a terrible and shameful thing to lead young women astray. Your advice will bring you either honor or disgrace. (601–06)

OLD WOMAN:

I won't hide myself in shame from gossiping tongues. What I have done confirms that I have only given advice. If anyone wants to contradict me about this, let him produce whatever it is that proves otherwise; let him come and face me with all he has; he can either win the day, or, if not, admit he's wrong and shut up. But good reasoning would stop him quickly in my favor; there's nothing he could say which would make sense. Just think: A nice, good looking young man, from a good family, with a lot of money. No, sweet love would be on our side. Let empty gossip be still; let people who mutter nasty things be quiet too. You can go your way without having to feel ashamed. (607–18)

GALATHEA:

Oh Good Lord, how someone in love can be tormented with indecision! Love and fear —love is so much of a burden— thrust you first this way and then that way! You can't make up your mind, and you're weary at all hours. What love chooses to do, fear does not permit. I just don't know what to do: I run around lost, hither and thither, and the wound inflicted by love gets worse. I'm overcome by love, although I try to resist. But as I do, it gets the better of me. I've been afflicted for a long time now; I'm worn out from a futile struggle. It's terrible to say so, but I would rather die than go on living like this. (619–28)

OLD WOMAN:

Just like a fire that flares up from its own force and a dispute that tends to get worse from anger and strife, so Venus tends to get harmful to herself from her own unrest; she makes for injuries with her useless back–and–forth. You can't, you know, put out the fire of love by trying to resist. The fire will die down by itself, if you don't put up a fight. You should obey the commands of Venus since you are now her soldier.[2] Don't let this restless struggling do you harm! If you act rashly right from the start you will lose your joy in life. You will hand yourself (and the one life you have in this world) over to an awful delusion. If your friend is not around, all you can do, day and night, is to imagine what he looks like. And he will do the same. That way each of you will only get to see the face of the other. Holding back like this will be the death of you. But I believe you still think you can easily get rid of these feelings of love. No! Getting away from him would only lead to an awful death. Take it easy while you're still young; enjoy the pleasures of life. People should treat themselves to a good time and have a little fun. You're alone now; why don't you come with me and relax for a while. (629–47)

---

[2] "soldier" ("miles"). A bit of incongruousness here. The author of the *Pamphilus* had obviously read the poetry of Ovid (see *Ars* I, vs. 132 for one instance of "miles"). But are we to suppose the go–between had also done this kind of reading?

OLD WOMAN (AT HER HOUSE WITH GALATHEA)

In this house of mine you can have fruits and nuts. There's almost always fruit growing in the yard. Why don't you go and enjoy yourself as much as you want. But what's that? Did someone try to break open the door? Was it a man or the wind? I think it was a man. It is a man, and he's looking at us through an opening! It's Pamphilus, I recognize his face quite well. He sure knows what to do: he's forcing back the bolt more and more. And now he's going to come in. But why do I just stand here and say nothing? Pamphilus, you nut, how dare you break my door, a door I bought with my own good money. What do you want? Did someone send you to me? If you've something to say, say it fast and go away. (648–60)

PAMPHILUS:

Galathea, you alone can bring me back to health; it has been so long; give me a thousand long kisses. But even with such kisses my burning love will not be satisfied. No, from simple games like these it will only become more intense. And now, here we are my one delight: I can wrap my arms around you. Yes, I can now embrace you, my dear sweet bundle of joy. What real good luck it was that caused me to come here, a place where I find the one I love most. (661–68)

OLD WOMAN:

My neighbor is calling; I'll go talk to her and then be right back. I'm afraid, you know, that she might come here. What are you shouting about? I'm on my way, I'm coming. Let me close my door. There's no one else at home and the house will be alone. Listen, I have some business to take care of. So tell me quickly what you want. I can't go with you anywhere. (669–74)

PAMPHILUS:

How wonderful, Galathea: our sweet love, our unspoiled youth, this place itself, summon us to enjoy ourselves to our hearts content. Venus too, that lascivious goddess, is forcing us to indulge in her joys; she is commanding us to do the things she stands for. Why the delay? Do I have to ask for her help in order to gain what I want? Galathea, please accept what I going to do. (675–80)

GALATHEA:

Pamphilus, get your hands off me! Your wasting your time. This is no good; what you want is impossible. Pamphilus, get your hands off me! You're offending me terribly. The old woman will soon be back. Pamphilus, get your hands off me. How awful, women have so little strength: how easy it is for you to keep my hands from resisting. Pamphilus, why are you hurting me? You are pressing too heavily against my breast. It's awful, it's terrible to treat me like this. Stop! I'm going to scream. What are you doing? How dare you undress me! Oh, I've been done in. When is that treacherous old woman going to come back? Please get up, the neighbors can hear what's going on. She did a rotten thing handing me over to you. You'll never catch me again in this place with you. That old woman will never trick me again as she did this time. Alright, you'll be the winner and have your way, although I did put up a good fight. But our love, of course, is over and finished. (681–96)

PAMPHILUS:

We've covered the course; we should rest now for a while to allow the horse to catch his breath. But how is it you're turning your eyes away from me, your lover? Why is your face drenched in tears? Yes, I'm completely at fault; I'll allow for any punishment you give me. Let it be even more than I deserve. Look, do what you want, I'll let you hit me and I'll just endure it. And yet the sin wasn't my fault. If you agree, we might look at it with a mind for fairness and justice. Should I be set free or judged guilty? Those fiery eyes you have, the whiteness of your flesh, your dignified face, your sweet speech, the way you hold me, your pleasant, playful kisses, these incited me to what I did, they were the start of it all. Love chased after me and urged me on by putting such things into my mind. I became dominated by an ever greater passion, I was on fire with fierce desire; I was provoked into committing the outrage. This furious passion overthrew my good sense; I became insensitive to pity. And you know, you too might justly be at fault for what I'm accused of. You might be the source and the cause of the wrongdoing. But there shouldn't be anger like this between two lovers. And if it happens to exist, then it shouldn't be allowed to last very long. A person in love should always tolerate the faults committed by the person he or she loves. Put up, then, with this burden for which we are both at fault. The old woman is going to come back. Please try not to look so sad. Don't let her think that your tears are the result of our having done something wrong. (697–722)

OLD WOMAN:
That woman kept me at her door while she babbled empty nonsense; she could outtalk Cicero himself. But Galathea, why are you ruining your pretty eyes with those tears? You look like you're in pain. How come? What did Pamphilus do to you while I was out? Galathea, please, tell me about it. (723–28)

GALATHEA:
That's just like you, to ask questions as if you didn't know what had happened. It was you who planned this! You can tell what a tree is like by its fruit. People can tell what you are like by what you do. Hardly had you given me the fruit and the nuts, when this Pamphilus of yours was at the door. Then your neighbor called you away so that there would be an opportunity for me to get robbed of my virginity. What good reason you had for taking your time outside the house! How cleverly you concealed your tricks! Your trickiness and immorality have done the job. Here I am, the hare on the run that fell into the trap. (729–40)

OLD WOMAN:
I'm unfairly accused —I've nothing to do with behavior like this— and I'll justify myself quite well in whatever way you want. The mere mention of this kind of offense doesn't really match my age, to say nothing of my actually concocting such things. If somehow an argument started up while you were having fun, would that be my fault? I was away. But no matter what, your fight has nothing to do with me; it was started by your silly love, not by me. But tell me anyway, Pamphilus, what happened. I don't want to be ignorant of the cause of this trouble. (741–50)

PAMPHILUS:
If you must know, I'm being accused of something that was not my fault. The anger I face is harsher than I deserve. But lovers

should always keep their intimacy a secret. We should be ashamed to speak of it, even if we don't feel a sense of shame. All that matters now is that you restrain your anger and this urge to argue. As for the rest, it should be strictly between us. (751–56)

GALATHEA:

Pamphilus, tell her what we did as if she didn't already know. We don't want her to be ignorant of how it took place, do we? She's asking you about what she herself advised you to do, as if she knew nothing. She wants it to seem she did nothing to harm me. You led me far astray with countless tricks, and yet the signs of trickery were obvious. And so it is that the fish, once caught, notices the bent hook; and the bird, once caught, perceives the traps set by men. What am I going to do now? I've been caught too. Shall I be a fugitive everywhere in the world? My parents are going to close their door to me, and rightly so. I'll be constantly on the move, here, there, everywhere, looking for a place to go. I'll be miserable, a poor woman without hope. (757–68)

OLD WOMAN:

A smart person would avoid a lot of grieving when nothing is gained by grieving. You should stay calm and accept a loss that no amount of ingenuity can ever get back. That's what happens when people are done in by a reckless love. In your case you would do well to control yourselves and watch out for problems as they come along. Get advice about what to do. Strife, as you know, is serious: it eats at the hearts of lovers and encourages them to strike at each other to no end. Make peace now and come together. It'll be good for you. She should be your wife (said to Pamphilus), he should be your husband (said to Galathea). And so it is. I've seen to it that you got what you wanted; I've made you happy. Don't forget me. (769–80)

END

APPENDIX B:
Pseudo–Ars Amatoria

If anyone should want to engage in love the right way, then let him begin in accordance with the teaching of my verse. Nobody should indulge in a terrible form of baseness and tempt a nun; she has held self–seeking in contempt and become allied to God; she is joined to Him like a married woman to her husband. To put a stain on her is rightly deemed an evil. Also a lover should not give of his substance to foul bordellos where they simply sell their flesh; no one can really have a good time there. When a prostitute submits she doesn't offer love; she doesn't even like what she does; she only wants to get what you have. (vv. 1–10)

There are many other women who are suitable for this kind of diversion. I can only speak highly of an effort to win a virgin or a widow, if one is available. The embrace of a virgin softens the hardest of hearts. It does away with sadness and brings heavenly joy to the spirit. Likewise the sweet love of a widow softens an arrogant disposition. She is skillful and goes about it better than the others. Yes, an attractive young woman, should there be one available, provides sweet joy; she inclines to light–hearted fun, she is open minded. If a young man is to learn to love these girls properly he should become familiar with my method. (11–20)

First of all he should search carefully for a woman to love.[1] Let

---

[1] *Pseudo–Ars* vv. 3–20 lack for a correspondence in the pertinent part of the *Libro* (the "Don Amor Lecture": sts. 423–575). One will notice, however, that vs. 21, where a correspondence resumes, constitutes a recommencement of sorts. We need not conclude, however, that vv. 3–20

him select someone he likes from among the many. He should look at her unabashedly and with a smile so that the girl will know she is the one he wants. Let him give thought above all to quality of character, type of family, and good looks. But he should not aim too high. Let him single out someone who is his social equal or only a little better than himself. The man who aims for the stars often goes nowhere except down and quickly too. (21–28)

He should then seek out the place where his ladylove always spends time; where the young woman tarries, there he should spread his nets. Here he should come in a light hearted mood; he should sing and sigh in her presence. If he is unable to do this he should resort to his imagination: he might put on a show of physical agility, or he might speak to her in gentle tones; whatever is pleasing, that he should do; something is sure to be effective. To have an excuse for turning up would be useful; her love will be intensified if he has a clever pretext ready. A woman likes a man who knows how to be cautious; she wants her relatives to remain unaware of what is going on. (29–38)

A go–between should be sought, a woman in whom each can confide. She should be a shrewd talker, saying what is pleasing to both. The young man should reward her so that she will go about this matter eagerly. But rather than actually give her something he should only make promises to her. (39–42)

When the go–between gets the beloved's ear, she should speak of love as sweetly as possible, starting off cleverly with something like this: "How beautiful you are, my dear, how wonderful you look. Would you mind if a fine young man in love felt attracted to you and had only good things to say about you? He's better than all the others; his manners show it. He would like very much— he even begs— to have a chat with you. Now that's something worthwhile: it speaks well for both of you. He's more ready to do what you want than any of your servants. He puts you above everything else; it's you he wants all the time. He sent me to you because you can

---

in the Latin poem were unknown to the Archpriest (albeit a direct transition from vs. 2 to 21 is smooth): he portrays the ladylove in the "Endrina" (sts. 576–891), the principal tale of seduction in the Spanish poem, as a widow.

count on me."[2] (43–52)

It may be that at first the young lady will have harsh words to offer. But she who was harsh will soon be soft. The go–between should speak sweetly to her; she should persuade her that the young man's intentions are good. Sometimes she should commend him, sometimes she should adulate her; she should have praises for both at the same time, first the one, then the other. (53–58)

But if the young woman is disinclined to yield for the moment, the go–between should return to the young man and explain in detail all that took place. He should not lose heart. Rather, he should make a more diligent effort, speaking often to his lady with nods and signs. How many times, in fact, does it happen that a lukewarm attraction, when skillfully provoked, causes a young girl without experience to burn with passion. (59–64)

The go–between should assail her often with blandishments and be slow to stop when the girl objects. What a woman does not permit she really desires; she wants to be constantly begged; sexual desire will overcome her will to resist; love will break it down. An iron bulk is wreaked by impure ingredients and a hard rock is bored through by the dripping of water. Thus it is that after a good deal of entreaty and the passing of time a young woman will freely agree to a conversation. (65–72)

For this purpose a meeting place privy to the two should be arranged; only the go–between should know what they are up to...[3] If, however, the square is crowded, as is frequently the case, and the lady is wont to talk to anyone she chooses, then the young man should greet her in soft tones, get closer, and say privately: "You are as brilliant as a heavenly star, your face is aglow with beauty. Here I am, your servant. Please let me to speak to you. If your dignity, your pureness, your good looks were judged for what they are, who could ever be your equal? Your striking beauty surpasses that of all other women; you would even outdo Venus were she not a goddess. Your hair is golden, your forehead is high and perfect.[4] Your brows

---

[2] That is, not to make the affaire public.

[3] Thiel postulates a lacuna here (between the verses numbered 74 and 75).

[4] At this point (beginning with verse 85) the author presents the reader

are dark, your eyes are cheery; I'm overcome by their every move: my heart is filled with joy; my love is impassioned. White and red together is the color of your cheeks. Your face, your nose, are in total harmony; you're a pleasure to look at. Your lips are perfect and flushed with a roselike color; if it were possible to join mine to yours, that would certainly be my desire. Your teeth are flawless and how splendidly white! When you laugh, your face brings joy to one and all. Your chin is graceful, your neck whiter than new snow; whenever I see it, my heart is warmed. And judging from your neck I can imagine how fair everything is that you hide under your dress. Your gorgeous nipples give a wonderful touch to each of your breasts. Oh, how easily I could take them into my hands. When you stand, you seem straight, graceful, fit for an embrace. Your arms and your hands, so full of life, deserve only praise. The rest of your body is all to your honor. You are finer than I could ever say. When I am unable to see you I die from a need to do so. And yet, when I gaze at you I perish. Such is the fire of my love. (73–106)

I am now in service to you. With your permission I present myself to you. Whatever you and you alone order me to do, that I will always do. If you were to give me an approving look or agree to accept my love, I would rejoice more than if someone gave me a kingdom. I request only this: that you acknowledge your loving servant, so that through you he may continue to live. Yes, you are my very life and being." (107–12)

Perhaps she, being clever, will have this to say in order to conceal outwardly with haughty words what she inwardly feels: "You are asking for something silly, young man; you waste your time by praising my body; even if I'm beautiful, why should you care about me? Go away, leave me alone immediately. Perhaps you thought I was "easy"? Don't ever talk to me like that again." (113–18)

The young man should then say: "Why, my dearest, are you causing my death? My death will be your fault. I ask for a great deal,

---

with a largely standard *descriptio pulchritudinis feminae*. The Archpriest's *descriptio* (sts, 431–435, 444–449), which differs, is in good part non-standard and unique to himself.

but it's worthy of being granted. If you could possibly love me, no harm would ever come to you." And she will then say in reply: "Frankly, I don't get readily impressed by anyone. But all right, since you are so persistent, I do rather like you." (119–24)

Whereupon, inclining his head and joyfully giving thanks, he should make a vow to be her servant forever. But that he might always serve her worthily and render her the tribute she deserves, he should propose giving a gift as a token of their new love (such gifts confirm the trust the two have in each other). He then should state that a kiss would be in order, but leave it to her to decide whether she wants to make the concession. When the gift has been given he should depart, happily showing gratitude and feeling sure of her love. (125–34)

Thereafter he should make it his business to find out when he might find his lady by herself in a place with no one else around. If he is unable to do this, the go–between should take charge—she will know how— and maneuver the lady to a locale "safe for playing games." Here the young man should turn up with a cheerful expression on his face. He should greet her, ask polite questions and utter her praises. And then, while they are talking and the woman is stirred by his adulation, he should gently touch her on the upper part of her dress (no girl is ever so narrow minded that, if touched, she would fail to react in good humor). If she avoids his touch, he should smile and persist, pressing his fingers on her hips and sides. But in all these things a gentle moderation should be exercised since nothing is good that is done without restraint. He should try to make the girl without experience enjoy herself. He should sweetly beg for her dear kisses. He should promise and swear that he will not ask for more and allege that these favors are enough for him. If she still does not yield and becomes angry, he should beg all the more for her kisses. But since modesty often causes girls to become upset, even to the point of denying to their husbands the kisses that are their due, the lover should not hesitate to force his arm around her neck and quickly take what she refuses to grant. (135–58)

When he finally joins his lips to her mouth, they should have long hard kisses. In the meantime his free hand should squeeze her breasts, and then feel her thigh and then her belly and so on back and forth. And after each lover has warmed up to the game, it is time for them to take off their clothes and get into position. The young man should use compulsion regardless of how much the girl may protest; if he stopped, she would suffer emotionally: a woman prefers to be overcome in a struggle rather than freely submit to an illicit act like a prostitute. Only from such women is it correct to simply ask for sex, since they commonly sell it to anyone for a price. Whoever wants sex and delays in using force after he has taken kisses, is a primitive person, never really worthy of love. (159–72)

If anyone has acquired a ladylove by means of my art he should seek help from the poet as to how to keep the love warm. A young man should try to converse with his lady often and stimulate her with endearing words. He should always be ready to wink or nod from a distance, if it would be risky to speak aloud up close. Whenever spirits are running high and the stomach is filled with an abundance of food and drink, he should eagerly approach her and ask for the pleasures of the flesh; this is the time when every man likes it most. (173–82)

He should strive to avoid boorishness to the best of his ability. Constant eating, for example, is usually something repugnant. He should keep his affair a secret so that his lady's reputation does not suffer. The result is a hidden love affair which is always more enjoyable. The pleasure he has had he should modestly seek to conceal. He should not make known the name of his mistress in public. He who loses his dear ladylove through his own fault should perpetually grieve over his crudity. (183–90)

APPENDIX C:
De Vetula

(*Verses 202 Through 728 of Book Two*)

For me there was only one countenance in all the realm of Nature. It was the one supreme glory of the feminine sex. It had the grace and charm of a virgin flower in bloom with natural and spontaneous qualities. In her the fine things of Nature were abundant to such a degree that I cannot recall so many qualities were ever assembled in one person. We might suppose that three sisters vied on her behalf: Nature, all powerful with her gifts, Grace, the giver of qualities that enhance, and unpredictable Fortune, she who is miserly with great things and generous with little things. But with this young woman the latter made an exception. For her, Fortune went beyond the usual and was kinder than to others: though she was already superior in type, Fortune gave to her a great abundance of wealth and nobility. Nature, for her part, gave an abundance of things that serve to elevate: excellence of body and spirit such that no one was equal to her in comportment and intelligence. Indeed, there was no one on the face of the earth equal to her for attractiveness, no one equal for excellence of speech. And to these qualities Grace, for her part, added so much as to make them seem even better. Her contribution was too great to judge objectively. But still, the final judgement must be based on sight: it would not be her speech nor her spirit which would win out in a contest: it would be her physical beauty. The victory would go unchallenged: her beauty could provoke none other than Hippolytus if he failed to look away. (vv. 202–29)

Why should I care to sing her praises in detail? Why should I bother to give to the various parts of her body the compliments they deserve? No description is good enough. If someone wanted me to describe them one by one, he ought to know that they are better than anything I am able to say. On the other hand, since it is a joy to recall such magnificent treasures, I shall in a brief way enumerate and speak of her individual charms (but only to the extent that an observing eye is allowed to range). They strive, to be sure, among themselves for preeminence. I intend, however, to present a general and impartial view: they will cease to struggle and instead array themselves in a peaceful succession; they will harmonize with each other in an overall splendor. (230–42)

Her thick hair envelops her elegant head from above with a royal glow.[1] Its radiant color rivals the flash of gold. But it has grown long with the passing of time and become a burden for the lady. So she binds it up, coercing it in a certain manner into a bundle. And yet the manner is such that some hairs remain free on her temples because of their shortness; they are intertwined in loose curls and flutter about with a capricious playful movement. Her ample forehead is a little convex: when smoothing it out with His hands God did not apply one of them adequately. Lilies do not surpass its brilliance, ivory is not its equal, nor is the white thistle. The curving dark line of her brows overlies on two sides the ridge of a slight declivity and establishes peace all around with a particular crescent shaped boundary. At the same time each brow stands out notably in its own right and separates the placement of the eyes from the forehead. Between them, however, where the nose continues on from the forehead, set deeper than the nose as well as the forehead and the brows, a certain small space is evident; it is free of hair and is similar to the privet for whiteness. Set below all this is an agreeable, cheerful extension which does service to her two eyes by enclosing the dark pupils with the protection of the lids. Its curving surface lends a pleasantness to her face when they conceal her eyes; they act, both together, as a cover, so that the eyes may suffer no unjust outrageous harm. When these partial spheres close, they do so with a certain gesture of lasciviousness, a token of

---

[1] In vs. 243 the author begins a *descriptio pulchritudinis feminae* (it continues on to 336). We have seen several samples of the theme already. This one stands out for an extraordinary verbosity.

the favors of love yet to be had. The brightness of her eyes is not dampened at all by tears around the edge. The nose does not extend excessively: it is neither too long nor too short; it is neither aquiline nor puglike; it shows no sign of an oblique tendency. The nostrils reveal no trace of inner elements in the openings, nor do they make for difficulty in breathing; they threaten no one with a disagreeable odor when she exhales. The peak of her cheeks rises gently up and outdoes the rind of apples with a bright red color. You would think that lilies were engaged in a struggle with roses: the rose red and the snow white combine to form one color, but in such a way that the red is overcome by the white. In her cheeks, moreover, dimples take form whenever the lady smiles; they add to her gracious face an amiability such that she might seem willing to grant anything to anyone who approaches her with a request. Her ears are sometimes covered by her moderately curly hair; but sometimes the ears act to hold the hair in place. All in all the sides of her face are small; but when she laughs, they assume a medium size. Her lips are reasonably full and unsurpassed for redness by cherries gathered in bright sunlight after a cloudburst. Since they are shaped a bit outwardly they seem to want to be ready to offer themselves for the taking of kisses. But when the lady is laughing, or just talking, or even eating, an astonishing array can be seen within her mouth. It is her teeth: they are brighter than the luster of polished silver and are set in perfect order, one after the other, straight, contiguous, firm, equal in dimension, but yet smallish. The lower part of her face, her agile chin, rises like a hill next to her neck and like a small mound next to her lips; but in both cases it does so gently. Her neck is as smooth as it is full; there is no rigid sinew, no puffy vein. Her complexion is free of any roughness; no blemish disfigures it; I would say it is whiter than snow if I may resort to an extreme of hyperbole. Her soft hand is fit to be extended when required. Her fingers are graceful, ample, well shaped, even, and of a proportionate length. The palms are white like milk, the nails are clear. (243–311)

The rest is barred to me: her dress covers it all. We may, however, draw conclusions, that is to say, by way of seen things move on to unseen things on the supposition that the latter are better than the former and are therefore describable. But since my knowledge rests on conjecture, we shall have to be content with brevity. I suppose that on the flat of her chest, rising like twin swellings, are her smallish breasts. They are firm, curvaceous, and seem to admit that they want to be squeezed in an embrace and want, of their own accord, to proceed to the man giving the embrace. Her long slim arms are fine, soft and full; the upper part descends in a straight line from beginning to end. Her torso is slender; her loins appear to be full and graceful in her girdle; her buttocks are modest but ample in extent. And then there is the movement of her legs, the bend in her knees, her small feet, well shaped and moving forward with an even gait. All these demonstrate the quality of that part which I desire so much. I think that no fashion, no apparel is more appropriate for her than to be without clothing. I wish I could see her nude just once, even if nothing else were forthcoming, and I were not permitted to touch her.[2] I have said little because words are not adequate for such matters: no description can make known how delightful it would be to make love to her or what joy there would be if she were willing. (312–36)

My eager eye devoured her desirable person and suggested to my avid self all sorts of thoughts. Boldly my heart began to hope that I could win her with words or gifts. Beyond my usual practice of words only, I prepared some gifts to give her in case my words would have no effect; with words I had so often entreated many a heart. Slowly the secret spark of love grew into an immense fire and was soon to take possession of my entire self. (337–45)

But the time and place for talking were not available since her mother and father, concerned lest she lend an ear to foolishness and be enticed away, were protecting her with a constant surveillance. What was I going to do? I had to look for a go–between who could speak to both of us in turn. She would have to be glib and free from suspicion, so that she would be allowed to approach us and no one would notice. (346–54)

While I was giving careful thought to these things, looking about the metropolis, evaluating many old women, and considering often and at length one thing after another, it happened that a certain poor old woman with a gift for gab turned up; she was a neighbor of my

---

[2] Cf. *Libro*, 435cd.

sister and frequently received something to eat in her house because of her pious appearance. In addition, she had once been my lady's devoted nursemaid. As I deemed her more useful than the others I went and spoke to her and set forth a proposal. I promised her a good deal provided she would keep things well concealed; but I also added some threats in case she betrayed me. At first she was evasive, arguing against the proposal and pointing out the dangers that could arise. "I would be in a jam," she said, "if her father found out about it. What would I do? What kind of punishment would I get. They might even kill me in some way or other. You too, you might deny that you put me up to it and that you paid me for it. I beg of you, by the gods above, make no further request like this. Please let me live out my old age in peace. I prefer to live in safety. Let my poverty suffice for me in the few remaining days which the fates have granted. I don't want to die a violent death for the sake of money. Let me avoid this: I prefer to live safe and sound rather than put up with so much worry because of your promises." (355–78)

But the more difficult she became, the more optimistic I became about the chances of winning the girl through her. I made a case for pursuing the matter, showing her that the father would uncover nothing unless she herself had done something amiss. As for the girl, someone so dear, so prudent, so considerate would surely not betray her. I noticed, however, that promises would have no effect, if I did not actually reward her with something. So I went against my usual procedure and enumerated the gifts I would give her and went on to promise even more. I was driven on by love, I was dragged on to my fateful end. Yes, I who formerly was unaccustomed to giving something now found myself unable to exercise restraint. I gave her a skin of wine, I gave her some wheat, I gave her some beans, I gave a chunk of meat, I gave a wimple, I gave a tunic, I gave a cloak, I gave a gown, I gave sandals, I gave three types of cloth for making underwear: the best of the latter would cover her arms and neck; her breast would have a piece of medium quality; her backside a shoddy piece; thus that part of her which stood to gain from anything would have the worst. She then called on the gods and swore by the furies, demanding her own destruction if her vow were not faithfully carried out. (379–98)

She frequently came and went and at first had a lot to say. She spoke of how often she made clever use of opportune moments, how often she shrank back from fear, how she gained entrance anyway, how she finally began to speak up, what pretext she was able to use for explaining the long absence from her nurseling, how she took a chance when she got around to her real purpose, and how the two then covered me with praise. She added, however, that she was rejected, albeit with politeness. In this way she sometimes caused me, in my misery, to become anxious. But at other times she held out a slim bit of hope. And whenever I reprimanded her by saying "you should have spoken in this way or that way," she assured me that she had so spoken and called upon the gods as witnesses that she was not lying. I did not know what to believe; I thought it was all a necessity; I believed her because I had no choice. In this way I was led astray by what she said for a considerable space of time. (399–414)

The truth comes out in the end. After this old woman —surely the biggest liar of them all— had led me on with so much deviousness and was no longer able to delay, she pretended quite ingeniously that my lady was ready to be had. "My dear man," she said, "you are the only truly trustworthy person in my life, a hope of sustenance, and a support in my old age. I have come to realize that the girl loves you above all others, but is not able to express it in any way. How terrible I am, how terrible I am; why must a decent young woman be tricked by me? But as it is, on a certain night, after her hair has been washed, I'll keep her away from her mother's bedroom in order to comb her hair. Then, when all the others are sound asleep, I'll have her lie down in a small room to the right as you come into the house (in the area where the housemaids otherwise sleep) saying that she should not go into the master bedroom and disturb her father's sleep. Then you, having made yourself ready, will come after the ninth hour, but only after it has become quite dark. I will unlock the door and dim the lamp. You will slowly and quietly open the door —holding it tightly so as not to make a racket— and go in. You will find her there naked in bed. Do your business quickly. Once you get possession of her, you will have no further problems." (415–36)

Eager and gullible I waited anxiously for the night on which we had agreed, albeit, at the same time, I was bothered by fears and second thoughts. Then, when the day before the stipulated evening had come, I washed a bit and trimmed my beard and body hair. After midday I relaxed for a while in order to get ready for the sleepless night I was going to have. Then I ate a few snacks and drank some wine. Thereafter I prepared to do some reading so that I would not fall asleep. I also took care to set the clock a little ahead to be sure of arriving on time.[3] (437–46)

As soon as the hour had come I doused my light. But I was not cautious going out and bumped into the door. My head hit the post, leaving me dazed and confused, and soiled by a flow of blood. Angry, I rushed forward and fell down the long staircase. I took an oath to the furies, since I thought I was driven on by them and only rarely does a misfortune like this happen just once. I also called —to no avail— upon the gods and made to them many a vow in the hope they would act in my favor. Yes, it is certainly the truth: only rarely does a misfortune happen just once: the clumsy servant who ordinarily takes care of the entrance was unaware of my intention and had closed the gate in the wrong way and jammed the bolt. Things like this, one after the other, were for me —nearly in a rage— the portents of something ill–fated. By now I had lost control of myself. Not caring at all about the noise, I broke the gate and opened it wide, thereby exposing all I owned to being stolen. I then went out; my misfortunes could not hold me back. I continued on to the house of my beloved which, if the bolt had been pulled back, I knew would be open to me. I needed merely to proceed with silence. I began to feel joyful as I entered the house from the side and, feeling my way along, made for the chamber and the bed. (447–68)

There she was, lying on a simple couch half asleep. You would never know how much of a sweet feeling began to go through me! It would be hard to say with how much desire my spirit was overcome. I avoided delay: all loss of time, however brief, seemed detrimental. I quickly took off my clothes. My own haste, however,

---

[3] Clock = *horologium*. But in this case the reference (one of the earliest) is apparently to a mechanical device, not an hourglass or clepsydra. The author disregarded the anachronism.

got in my way: though I hurried, wanting to avoid losing time, I still lost time. Finally, having gotten undressed, I took hold of the naked girl and held her tight. She was not able to turn at all; she was totally unable to move. The modesty of a virgin is such that she wishes to be overwhelmed like this. She considers herself as spared an offense if she is not spared at all. Such would have been the proper procedure with my young virgin if she had been the one who was there with me. It was fitting that Semele be approached by a lustful Jupiter in this fashion. But the approach would not have been right in the case of Beroe. (469–485).

How awful! Of all the sweet feeling which had come over me, little now remained. I found the opposite of my desire. The sound of the cithara was turned into a sound of mourning, the hope of delight was turned into numbness, the fiery torch of love went out. If before there had been something which aroused my passion to the point of fury, it suddenly languished and fell dead. My strength ebbed, all my limbs became sluggish. Who would think that a girl who recently became sixteen could get old so fast? Never has a rose shriveled in so short a time. I have sung of forms altered into new bodies. But no more marvelous change can be found than this one. To think that in such a short space of time a girl like her would change into an old woman like this. (486–99)

It was terrible: how unlike the limbs of a young woman were these limbs: the jerky movement of her frame, her sinewy neck, her scrawny shoulders were suggestive of an elderly woman. Her tough breast of stretched leather was not really a breast but a shepherd's bag, empty and slack. Her stomach had been furrowed by a plow, her buttocks were dry and lean, her legs were coarse, her swollen knees were as hard as a diamond. The weak confused motion of the ensemble was like that of an old woman. Pulling myself together I got up and resolved to go at her with my sword. But the good name of my young lady came to mind: so as not to expose her to a scandal I restrained myself. All hope of possessing her had come, however, to an end. I took no action, and my love, though suppressed, was able to compensate for my intense suffering. It was no easy thing that I should love someone and have no hope. Indeed it is the hardest of tests. But it shows that I am worthy of being loved, I who can love and do so without hope of fulfillment. Though I did not get the woman who might have responded to my affection, I still retained a warm feeling towards her since I knew she was not at fault. (500–20)

At wits end I could scarcely get hold of my clothing. But I did, and went out the door, as sad now as I had been joyful when I came in. Upon arriving home I was barely able to lock the main entrance and my personal chamber. Without turning on lights I returned to my couch. Sorrowfully, I reflected on what would be a fitting retribution for her. But I could come upon nothing suitable. If she were to die now, her death would be a swift and easy punishment. Let her live on, rather, and pay for the atrocious act over a long period of time.[4] Let her be wretched, and not find a pitying hand to help her; if something is given to her, let it be paltry and bad; let her eat no bread unless it was produced with rotten grain; let her eat no meat except that which is aged or putrid; let her eat no fish which is not contaminated by a stench in all parts; let her partake of no wine unless it is pasty or sour; may she cough for all eternity; may gout wear down her joints; may she have a fever, and while she burns, suffer from an unquenchable thirst; may she have persistent chills and also strong heat spells; if possible, may she have both at the same time, or at least one right after the other; may she weep continually, and have perpetual tears in her eyes; may she have sudden fits of sobbing and sighs and have these often and repeatedly; may she gasp for breath while racked with stiffness; may she belch out a foul smell; may she be unable to clear her nose, and may sordid matter flow down into her; may she not spit it out, but swallow it and then regurgitate; may her bladder and rectum not contain her urine or waste: rather, let there be a constant flow back and forth. But enough of this. After that awful act of hers it would be impossible to have so many misfortunes that they serve as a fitting punishment. (521–49)

As I was getting over my sorrow, the pain was renewed: the girl was given in marriage, and her spouse, a man of status, took her a long way off. It was a place to which I had no reason to go. In addition, I had not found out if my frustrated sentiments had become known to her and I had no occasion for making inquiries. I was extremely upset.

---

[4] From this point, vs. 529 and on to 549, the author, in spite of his learning, demonstrates an extraordinary capacity for coarseness. As indicated elsewhere the poem contains a little something for everyone.

O you, whoever you are, as you take away my lady, you take away, yes you do, my heart as well. But the marriage is none of my business: I cannot step forth and forbid her father to marry off his daughter as he chooses. Still she belongs to me in a special and secret fashion: though she cannot be joined to me, I will not cease to be joined to her in spirit. (550–62)

As it was, after she had been married for some twenty years and was worn out with frequent childbirth (her face in particular had suffered loss) the fates ordered that her spouse end his days. So she decided to return to her parents' house, but did so leaving behind her eldest son and an agent to see to the inheritance. A crowd of relatives and friends came out to meet her. Getting well ahead of the others, I went to her and related briefly and in order what had happened. Smiling, she said: "I certainly remember, but I thought you had made a change in favor of the old woman." I took an oath to the gods that I had not made such a change. "But," she said, "what use is it to bring up all this now? Are we not both rather old and hardly up to an affaire?" I was going to persist, but could add nothing suitable as the crowd of wellwishers was approaching. (563–79)

On a certain morning as I happened to be going through some of my books I came to the passage which says "Particularly so, if she is past her prime," et cetera.[5] I laughed and at the same time I saw through a window that my beloved was coming along. For those favored by fortune many things seem to count as omens. She was on her way to visit the laurel tree and the tripod stool of the oracle and would presently pass by my house and the enclosure of the Temple of the Sun (the Palatine Hill being off to the left). I went out to meet her and was eager to put my household at her disposal on the supposition she might find my dwelling pleasant or simply relax and enjoy herself in the relative quiet. She replied: "This is not the time to do much talking, but I shall keep in mind to send you a trustworthy intermediary when opportune." (580–93)

At a later point a well spoken handmaid came to me from my lady. She brought with her some valuable jewelry made up of gold and

---

[5] Ovid is represented as quoting one of his own verses (*Ars amatoria* II, 665) to himself.

precious stones fashioned together with remarkable workmanship. "These," she said, "belong to my mistress. Her agent dispatched them to her recently in return for cash. But since we don't have so much currency in the house, she is sending them to the dealers as security for a loan. I am aware, however, that she rather likes you, and it occurred to me to proceed otherwise. But I don't want her to know I came here because of you, and I don't want you to think she is attracted to you because of what you own. Put your trust in this plan of mine; it will be effective. I appreciate the fact that you are a sensible person. If you have some cash, why don't you take these things and then give them back to her. I'll pretend you saw me returning from the bank and inquired why I went there.[6] After you learned the cause you wanted to be of help. In this way you can steal her heart. Take it from me: she'll be grateful to you." I would have been embarrassed not to do it. And so I affixed my seal to the box filled with the valuables while at the same time declining to retain them. (594–613)

When, after five days had elapsed and it was evident that no messenger had come back, I said to myself: "It can be, since money can incite greed, that the servant did not say she had gotten money from me. An opportunity to commit a theft can often be hard to resist, and this was a real chance for theft. If the woman had indeed stolen the money she would seek to avoid getting caught and would have told her mistress not to talk to me so that I could not ask if the funds had reached her intact. But if I inquire anyway, what would happen if she simply denies it? I don't have witnesses, and no possibility of producing witnesses. I should have kept the security: then she would have been obliged to declare to whom she had given it, and admit as well that she had done so in exchange for money. Otherwise, presumably, she would not have left it with someone. But as it was, I wanted to have a thorough talk with my lady so that she would reach a decision on me as a lover. Oh, if only she were sorry that she had been so insensitive towards me at the start. Yes, if only she were sorry. Of revenge as such, I have no need, even if lovers exist who get

---

[6] Part of the plan, apparently, is a pretense that the loan was refused at the bank.

pleasure from that sort of thing. (614–33)

While I was reflecting along these lines the problem solved itself with no further ado. The handmaid turned up with a smile on her face. "How fortunate you are," she stated, "your dearest sends you greetings, and says that what you did is admirable, the gesture even more than the deed. She gratefully sends her thanks." I am returning the security so that you might know she does not want you only for what you have, but rather for you yourself. She wants you to decide whether to keep it in your possession, or come and give it back and take possession of her. She will make good on the loan as quickly as possible —have no doubt— and to show she means it, wants to give a noble form of interest: interest by means of the body, the kind that pleases lovers. Such arrangements can hardly be called demanding. Come, then, tonight, but make it late. Also, there should be no fourth party as a witness: she wants no fourth person present. Two people, however, are insufficient: a third person will have to be there. I myself will suffice to serve the interests of the two of you. This hand will act to give you to her and her to you. (634–51)

After saying this and returning the security to me— against my will— she left. So I came in the night to my lady's house and brought the jewels with me. I did not want to keep them because I knew I could always trust her (she had, after all, returned them). Having been proven honest in one respect, she would show herself just as trustworthy in various others. If trust is not destroyed by mendacity it tends to persist. To be sure, a good many persons readily return something with a certain value in order to gain an increase in the trust that others have in them. But here we have a difference: once it is given, this one thing outweighs many other things.[7] (652–60)

When I got there the maid was ready for me at the door. She let me in and brought me directly to the bed. Since I had once been tricked by a deceitful woman I reached out to test this woman and found that every part of her was as it ought to be: her forehead, her eyes, her nose, her lips, her chin. I heard her give a laugh. Whereupon I lunged at her and gave her passionate kisses. Need I say more? Soon

---

[7] The sense is not immediately clear: "this one thing" ("hoc unum") would seem to refer to the lady's sexual favors.

undressed, I was received with great tenderness. I was in a state of total delight, I was caught up in my love of old. It was a joy to recall what she had been. And now she was showing me how intact she still was in spite of the wear of time. Never was any matron of so many years more fit than she, especially after giving birth so often. No one was more wholesome, or had a better fragrance about herself. I shall be silent about the rest. Let it be enough to say that we were as one in bed and each strove to satisfy the other. I went out just as I had been received: in peace. (661–75)

But then a fresh disturbance arose within me. It had the character of a serious dispute, a fierce anger, a terrible antagonism, an ongoing rancor, an awful commotion, a bitter contest, a difficult debate to which no solution could put a halt. Whenever in a moment of quiet I gave thought or consideration to what Fortune had given me or what pure chance had taken away, I would be drawn about at random, hither and thither, first rejoicing that in the end I had won out beyond my expectations, but then getting depressed when I recalled how late was my victory and how the ravages of old age would in no wise be reversed. My desire of long duration would increase my joy, but an unyielding sense of futility would increase my depression. And yet the sense of futility could not do away with the joy, nor could the desire eliminate the pain. They acted constantly as counterparts though no peace was possible between them. They competed, but neither was able to get the better of the other. Placed on a scale, neither could tip the balance in its favor. (676–93)

Who can teach me to show thanks to my lady such that I would seem neither ungrateful nor go to excess with gratitude? That is what I must do: show a mixed form of gratitude: let it be something neither very good nor something very bad; something indeed, but only to a limited extent.[8] If it is something good, let it yet be unpleasant; if it is something bad, let it yet be pleasing. May she not be so sad that she would have no inner joy; may she not be so glad that she would have no inner sorrow. If she should receive an honor, if she should receive an affront —may something negative not lack for something positive—

---

[8] Again a litany of hostile or contentious utterances. The author seems to have a penchant for this kind of verbal display.

let it quickly be forgotten. If she were to suffer an injury, may it be alleviated in part. If she were to acquire some benefit may she lose it in part. If she should ever be fearful, may she also be tranquil. If she should have peace of mind may she not be free from fear. May she not, however, fall gravely ill: one ultimate sickness will suffice: the old age which is bound to come over her. (694–708)

Mixed gratitude like this is what any ladylove deserves who refuses to give herself to her lover until she becomes older. Accordingly, may my own lady have neither better nor worse than the others, if what had happened was her fault. And it does seem that it was, since she admitted that she remembered what the old woman had done. Unless she had been aware beforehand of the old woman's intention she would not have acknowledged afterwards that she recalled the event. (709–15)

We should not, however, associate any and every elderly woman with such doings. Any woman who has gotten old in my possession will seem to me forever young. This one, however, since she did not get old with me is a source of both pleasure and displeasure. It is a joy to have had her. And yet, though she will always have the allure of a fine young girl, it will be hard not to identify her with aging as well. Let me stress that for me an old woman is someone who did not get old with me. Yes, let it be clear: those who have gotten older with me will forever be young.[9] In any case I do not intend to seek a younger woman. A fear I have that she could be worse than the girl before her is greater than any hope I have she could be better. That is especially true if she assumes I am now less virile than I used to be and starts up talk to the effect that: "What a fool this geezer is making of himself!" (716–28)

END OF BOOK TWO

---

[9] "Ovid" is apparently referring to former ladyloves who have since become elderly.

Bibliography of Cited Editions and Studies

EDITIONS
(For editions of the *Libro de buen amor* see entries under both
ARCIPRESTE DE HITA and JUAN RUIZ)

Andreæ Capellani. *De amore*. 1892. Ed. E. Trojel. Munich: Eidos Verlag,
1964.

Andreas Capellanus. *The Art of Courtly Love*. Trans. John Jay Parry. New
York: Columbia University Press, 1941.

Arcipreste de Hita. *Libro de buen amor*. Ed. María Brey Mariño. Madrid:
Editorial Castalia, 1968 (a modernized text but with notes and
commentary of interest).

———. *Libro de buen amor*. 1913. 2 vols. Ed. Julio Cejador y Frauca.
Madrid: Espasa Calpe, 1967.

———. *Libro de buen amor*. Ed. Manuel Criado de Val and Eric W. Naylor.
2nd ed. Madrid: Consejo Superior de Investigaciones Científicas, 1972
(a transcription of the three principal manuscripts).

———. *Libro de buen amor*. Ed. G. B. Gybbon-Monypenny. Madrid:
Editorial Castalia, 1988.

Baudry de Bourgueil. *Les Œuvres poétiques de Baudri de Bourgueil*. Ed.
Phyllis Abrahams. Paris: Librairie Ancienne Honoré Champion, 1926.

Boncompagno da Signa. *Rota Veneris*. Trans. Joseph Purkart. Delmar:
Scholar's Facsimiles and Reprints, 1975.

———. *Rota Veneris*. Ed. Carl Sutter. In *Aus Leben und Schriften des
Magisters Boncompagno*. Freiburg: Akademische Verlagsbuchhandlung
von J. C. B. Mohr, 1894.

Drouart La Vache. *Li Livres d'amours*. Ed. Robert Bossuat. Paris: Librairie
Ancienne Honoré Champion, 1926.

Les Fabulistes latins. 5 vols. Ed. Leopold Hervieux. Paris: Librairie de
Firmin-Didot, 1894.

Facetus. Ed. Alfred Morel-Fatio. "Mélanges de littérature catalane."
Romania. XV (1886): pp. 192-235.

Gonzalo de Berceo. *Los milagros de Nuestra Señora*. Ed. Brian Dutton. London: Tamesis Books, 1971.

Ibn Hazm de Córdoba. *El collar de la paloma*. Trans. Emilio García Gómez. 2nd ed. Madrid: Alianza Editorial, 1967.

———. *The Dove's Neck-Ring*. Trans. A. R. Nykl. Paris: Librairie Orientaliste Paul Geuthner, 1931.

Juan Ruiz. *Libro de buen amor*. Ed. Alberto Blecua. Madrid: Ediciones Cátedra, 1992.

———. *Libro de buen amor*. Ed. Giorgio Chiarini. Milan: Riccardo Ricciardi, 1964.

———. *Libro de buen amor*. Ed. Joan Corominas. Madrid: Editorial Gredos, 1967.

———. *Libro de buen amor*. Ed. Jacques Joset. Madrid: Altea, Taurus, Alfaguara, 1990.

———. *Libro de buen amor*. 1941. Ed. María Rosa Lida de Malkiel. Buenos Aires: EUDEBA, 1973 (a partial edition but with notes and commentary of interest).

———. *Libro de buen amor*. Ed. Raymond Willis. Princeton: Princeton University Press, 1972.

Matthew of Vendôme. *Ars versificatoria*. Ed. Edmond Faral. In *Les Arts poétiques du XIIe et du XIIIe siècle*. Paris: Librairie Honoré Champion, 1958. pp. 109–93.

———. Untitled collection of verse epistles edited and published by W. Wattenbach under the designation "Ein poetischer Briefsteller von Matthæus von Vendôme." *Sitzungsberichte der bayerischen Akademie der Wissenschaften*. Nov. (1872): pp. 561–631 (of special relevance are 607–10).

Ovid. *Ars amatoria*. Trans. J. H. Mozley. In *The Art of Love and Other Poems*. Cambridge: Harvard University Press, 1962, pp. 12–175.

———. *Heroides and Amores*. Trans. Grant Showerman. London: William Heinemann, 1921.

———. *Remedia amoris*. Trans. J. H. Mozley. *In The Art of Love and Other Poems*. Cambridge: Harvard University Press, 1962, pp. 178–273.

Pamphilus. Ed. Franz G. Becker. In Pamphilus, *Prolegomena zum* Pamphilus *und kritische Textausgabe*. Ratingen: A. Henn Verlag, 1972.

———. Ed. Adolfo Bonilla y San Martín. "Una comedia latina de la Edad Media: El "Liber Pamphili." *Boletín de la Real Academia de la Historia*, 70 (1917), pp. 395–467.

———. Ed. Eugène Evesque. In *La "Comédie" latine en France*. Comp. Gustave Cohen. 2 vols. Paris: Société d'Édition "Les Belles-Lettres," 1931, II, pp. 194–223.

———. Trans. Thomas J. Garbaty. *"Pamphilus, De Amore*: An Introduction and Translation." *Chaucer Review*, 2 (1967), 108–34.

Pseudo–Ars amatoria. Ed. Erich Joseph Thiel. "Mittellateinische Nachdichtungen von Ovids *"Ars amatoria"* und *"Remedia amoris." Mittellateinisches Jahrbuch*. V (1968): pp. 168–77.

Pseudo–Cato. *Dicta Catonis*. In *Minor Latin Poets*. 1934. Trans. J. Wight Duff and Arnold. M. Duff. Cambridge: Harvard University Press, 1968. pp. 592–639.

Pseudo–Ovidius De Vetula. Ed. Paul Klopsch. Leiden: E. J. Brill, 1967.

Pseudo–Remedia Amoris. Ed. Erich Joseph Thiel. "Mittellateinische Nachdichtungen von Ovids *"Ars amatoria"* und *"Remedia amoris." Mittellateinisches Jahrbuch*. V (1968): pp. 177–80.

Zabara, Joseph Ben Meir. *The Book of Delight*. Trans. Moses Hades. New York: Columbia University Press, 1932.

STUDIES

Allen, Peter L. *The Art of Love: Amatory Fiction from Ovid to* The Romance of the Rose. Philadelphia: University of Pennsylvania Press, 1992.

Blumenthal, Wilfried. "Untersuchungen zur Komödie "Pamphilus." *Mittellateinisches Jahrbuch*." 11, (1976): pp. 224–311.

Born, Lester K. "Ovid and Allegory." *Speculum*. (1934): pp. 362–79.

Buceta, Erasmo. "La 'Política' de Aristóteles, fuente de unos versos del *Libro de buen amor." Revista de filología española*. XII (1925): pp. 56–60.

Castro, Américo. *España en su historia. Cristianos, moros y judíos*. Buenos Aires: Editorial Losada, 1948.

Creizenach, Wilhelm. *Geschichte des neueren Dramas*. 3 vols. 2nd ed. Halle: S. M. Niemeyer, 1911–23.

Curtius, Ernst Robert. *European Literature and the Latin Middle Ages*. Trans. Willard R. Trask. Princeton: Princeton University Press, 1953.

Dagenais, John. *The Ethics of Reading in Manuscript Culture: Glossing the* Libro de buen amor. Princeton: Princeton University Press, 1994.

Dwyer, Richard A. "Ovid in the Middle Ages." In *Dictionary of the Middle Ages*. 13 vols. Ed. Joseph R. Strayer. New York: Charles Scribner's Sons, 1987.

Faral, Edmond. *Les Arts poétiques du XIIe et du XIIIe siècle*. Paris: Librairie Honoré Champion, 1958.

Guzmán, Jorge. *Una constante didáctico–moral del* Libro de buen amor. 2nd ed. Santiago de Chile: EDEH, 1980.

Gybbon–Monypenny, G. B. "Autobiography in the *Libro de buen amor* in the light of some literary comparisons." *Bulletin of Hispanic Studies.* XXXIV (1957): pp. 63–78.

———. G. B. " 'Dixe la por te dar ensiempro:' Juan Ruiz's Adaptation of the *Pamphilus.*" In *Libro de buen amor Studies.* Ed. G. B. Gybbon–Monypenny. London: Támesis, 1970, pp. 123–47.

Lecoy, Felix. *Recherches sur le Libro de buen amor.* Paris: Librairie E. Droz, 1938.

Lea, Henry Charles. *History of Sacerdotal Celibacy in the Christian Church.* 2 vols. London: Williams and Norgate, 1907.

Lehmann, Paul. *Pseudo–Antike Literatur des Mittelalters.* Darmstadt: Wissenschaftliche Buchgesellschaft, 1964.

Leo, Ulrich. *Zur dichterischen Originalität des Arcipreste de Hita.* Frankfurt: V. Klostermann, 1958.

Lida de Malkiel, María Rosa. *Dos obras maestras españolas*: El Libro de buen amor y La Celestina. 2nd ed. Buenos Aires: Editorial Universitaria de Buenos Aires, 1966.

———. *Estudios de literatura española y comparada.* 2nd ed. Buenos Aires: Editorial Universitaria de Buenos Aires, 1969.

Menéndez Pidal, Ramón. *Poesía juglaresca y orígenes de las literaturas románicas.* 6th ed. Madrid: Instituto de Estudios Políticos, 1957.

Mott, Lewis Freeman. *The System of Courtly Love.* New York: Haskell House, 1965.

Paetow, Louis John. *The Arts Course at Medieval Universities with Special Reference to Grammar and Rhetoric.* Urbana Champaign: University of Illinois, 1910.

Phillips, Gail A. *The Imagery of the Libro de buen amor.* Madison: H.S.M.S., 1983.

Raby, F. J. E. *A History of Secular Latin Poetry in the Middle Ages.* 2 vols. Oxford: Clarendon Press, 1957.

Rico, Francisco. "Sobre el origen de la autobiografía en el *Libro de buen amor.*" *Anuario de estudios medievales.* 4 (1967): pp. 301–25.

Riquer, Martín. "Ordenación de estrofas en el *Libro de buen amor.*" *Boletín de la Real Academia Española.* 47, (1967): pp. 115–24.

Schevill, Rudolph. *Ovid and the Renascence in Spain.* Berkeley: University of California, 1913.

Schloesser, Felix. *Andreas Capellanus, seine Minnelehre und das christliche Weltbild um 1200.* Bonn: H. Bouvier u. Co. Verlag, 1960.

Seidenspinner–Nuñez, Dayle. *The Allegory of Good Love: Parodic Perspectivism in the Libro de buen amor.* Berkeley: University of California Press, 1981.

Traube, Ludwig. *Einleitung in die lateinische Philologie des Mittelalters.* 1911. Munich: Verlag C. H. Beck, 1965.

Webber, Edwin J. "Juan Ruiz and Ovid." *Romance Notes.* II, Fall (1960): pp. 54–57.

Wilkinson, L. P. *Ovid Recalled.* Cambridge: The University Press, 1955.

Zahareas, Anthony N. *The Art of Juan Ruiz, Archpriest of Hita.* Madrid: Estudios de Literatura Española, 1965.

Zinberg, Israel. *A History of Jewish Literature.* 12 vols. Trans. Bernard Martin. Cleveland: The Press of Case Western Reserve University, 1972.

Index